# KEY
# TO
# HEAVEN

Stella Hermoine Howell

First Edition 2013
Reprinted 2015

Second Edition 2017 Published by FeedARead.com


Non - religious
Channelled Spiritual Lessons including practical techniques
for Eternal Life & Ascension into Heaven

© YAHVAH BOOKS
www.ecotrace.co.uk Stella@ecotrace.co.uk
(ECO = Ecological Cosmological Oceans)©
4 Eccles Court, Tetbury, Gloucester GL8 8EH United Kingdom
Mobile UK (0)7831 220631

This Channelled Book is rightly dedicated to
the Sole Almighty Creator YAHVAH
Who has made it possible to disclose these
Hidden Ancient Mysteries to modern Humanity

These Sacred Teachings of Truth are not available
in a single book through any other source.

The Most Powerful name YAHVAH has been
systematically removed globally, through centuries from
all places of worship and scriptures.

In these End Hours,
we can now prove that it is the Almighty Creator
And not a past Messiah
Who is the Alpha & the Omega
The Beginning & the End

HE who IS
HE who WAS
HE who will ALWAYS BE
Blessed is HE who Reigns forever

'Y A H V A H'

No man, no technology, no power can change
HE who is the Alpha & the Omega

## About the Author

Due to the unusual contents in this book, I outline a synopsis of my Professional career, confirming that I am of sound mind.

I am referred to by Governments, as a visionary and innovator, for which I received several accolades including Grant funding. I also assisted in setting a question for Diana Princess of Wales Enquiry.

In 1980 I predicted to the Ministry of Agriculture, Food and Fisheries (MAFF) the escalation of global population loosing their memories commencing in the UK, effecting all ages.

You may be aware that since 2014 individuals of varying ages were diagnosed with Alzheimer's due to similar symptoms though not Alzheimer's. This is on the increase.

With funding, I could assist cure/heal patients of various diseases live a healthy life. Recently having cured a disabled mature male I not only received threatening telephone calls but also had Police and a Social Worker knock on my door.

The wrong I had done was to reduce the sale of the Pharmaceutical network as well as NHS services. This is part of what politicians refer to as the Economy. Pharmaceuticals are not manufactured to cure. The industry would not exist with Healthy people who do not require drugs. Pharmaceuticals must have a detrimental effect to enhance the Economy.

My sole method of healing is invoking Cosmic Power. The book teaches you the method which is possible for everyone. This is Secret Ancient Wisdom.

My appointments include that with the European Commission as an 'Independent' Expert Analyst. I was also a Peer Reviewer by the National Health Service UK (NHS).

Alongside I founded a couple of Limited Companies of which I was Managing Director.

I hold a Patent and received several accolades as an 'Outstanding Individual' for 'Innovation' Patenting my unrivalled Proprietary Branded products as well as services.

My passion is in Teaching Ancient Mysteries of Mother Earth, Cosmology, the Mystical Human Body, Healing, Curing & all things related. It is possible for further Channelled books to be released on these and other subjects not covered by others.

I have no power of my own.

I am only the 'Host' for the Almighty Creator to create awareness of His Sacred Name, His Natural Law, His Creations and the purpose of our Life on Earth, thereby achieving Justice to the Almighty Creator as well as to Humanity

All my work is Free.
I do not sell anything for Profit.

Peace to your Mind for purchasing this book.
It is the best investment that you have ever made, this I assure you.

Should you wish to attend my Open Days, events, classes or other normally in Tetbury, Gloucestershire, UK kindly contact me.

Peace be with you.

Stella Hermoine Howell
www.ecotrace.co.uk
Stella@ecotrace.co.uk
Mobile UK (0)7831 220631

# Table of Contents

## The Sole ALMIGHTY CREATOR
## The Sole UNIVERSAL BEING
## The Sole Alpha & Omega
## is
## 'Y A H V A H'

YAHVAH   CREATED    all Life everywhere –
on Mother Earth,
in the Atmosphere,
in Water,
Underground,
in the Cosmos
much more than we are capable of comprehending.

YAHVAH   is   NOT   a   god*

YAHVAH is the Universal CREATOR

YAHVAH   CREATED   gods*

YAHVAH   ALONE   can   CREATE

YAHVAH   ALONE   was   WORSHIPPED   during   the VEDIC AGE
(details in Lesson 2).

YAHVAH   ALONE   must   be   WORSHIPED for global Peace &
Prosperity.

**YAHVAH,** the **Most Powerful Name** has been systematically
**removed** internationally from
**All places of worship**
All modern Scriptures & so called Holy Books

The word *'god' is only a title for example, similar to Mr or Mrs or Lord or Sir etc.

Unless one invokes a name for instance in a document, it is a circular, available to all or even rejected by all.
Who do you pray to?

If you asked me the same question I would answer, to the Almighty Creator who gives me Life.

Does your priest use the word 'god*'?

Who does your priest invoke when he says god*?

Will your Priest invoke 'YAHVAH' the Almighty Creator?

It is vital to know the name of the 'lord' 'god*' invoked.

There are both evil as well as good 'gods*' or deities or angels etc.

Evil 'gods*' support lies, deceit, war, injustice to name a few.

Invoking Evil 'gods*' of darkness brings upon sickness, disease, misfortune, unhappiness and eventual death.

Evil 'gods*' are 'satan', 'lucifer' & their teams who are also referred to as 'baal'. Evil gods* are thirsty for Human & Animal blood sacrifice (including fish).

You quench the thirst of blood seeking Evil gods* each time you purchase or eat Flesh & Blood of innocent animals.

Invoking the Almighty Creator,
Who is of Love, Peace, Justice
Bestows upon you
Perfect' Health, Happiness, Peace
Regeneration of your Physical Body, reversing the ageing process
& much more

10

The Almighty Creator YAHVAH is of Pure Love
HE Loves His entire Creations
HE Loves You
The Almighty Creator abhors Animal Sacrifice.

## The Sacred Name YAHVAH

## VEDIC AGE was the First Age of Human Beings

### YAHVAH the Sacred name

### YAHVAH the most Powerful Name

### is the Name of the Almighty Creator.

YAHVAH is inscribed in the **Rigg Vedas.**
**Rigg Vedas date back to c.830 BC.**

**Rigg Vedas** are part of the **Vedas** compiled during the **Vedic Age.**

The **Vedas** are the **First Holy Scriptures** ever written.
**Vedas** are **never updated** because they are **original & of Truth.**

**Vedic Scriptures** are written in **Sanskrit.**
**Sanskrit** is the **First Language.**

Today, modern **Sanskrit** does **NOT** contain the Ancient Original Sanskrit letters. Perhaps one of the forthcoming YAHVAH channelled Books will be on **Ancient Sanskrit** and its teachings.

In the **Rigg Veda, YAHVAH** is written **41 times** in **33 Hymns**
There are **1028 Hymns** in the **Rigg Vedas.**

In the **VEDAS** the **Sacred** all **Powerful name** is mentioned as:

### YAHVA, YAHVAH, YHVH

Observe YAHVA, YAHVAH, YHVH all have 'V' not 'W' in the VEDAS.

YAHVA is mentioned **21** times in the **Rig Vedas**

**YAHVI** is mentioned **20** times

YAHVL is mentioned **16** times

**Rigg Veda** states **YAHVAH** is the:

'VERY NAME of the CREATOR'

This is **INSCRIBED** as a **EPITHET**

**YAHVAH ALONE** was worshipped during the **Vedic Age** of **Prosperity.**

During this Age Human Beings ate Food only from Trees & Plants.

Human Beings never slaughtered nor ate any animal nor fish or dairy of any sort. Their DNA was entirely Human and not animal resulting also in their high intellect and spirituality.

Their diet consisted of raw food. No **FIRE** was used for **cooking.** Neither was there any requirement for unnatural items such as cutlery nor crockery.

## Yajur Veda xvii.19

**Yajur Veda** with reference to **'YAHVAH'** the **Almighty Creator states:**

"Being all VISION,
all POWER,
all MOTION in HIMSELF,
HE sustains with HIS POWER the WHOLE UNIVERSE
HIMSELF being ONE alone"

## Yajur xiv.31 & Shatapatha Brahmana States :

"The CREATOR of all,
the RULER of the Universe,
the SUSTAINER of ALL, holds
ALL things by 33 devatas"
**33 Devatas** perform their proper **functions as existing:**

"IN HIM & BY HIM

the ONE & ONLY CREATOR YAHVAH"


**33 Devatas have their play in the ALMIGHTY CREATOR**

**Devatas** are Divine Spirit Beings, some are Archetypes.

Through the Almighty Creator they exercise their beneficial influences attracting useful properties

HE ALONE is the ALL &
ALL of ALL the DEVATAS


All **33 Devatas OWE** their **Birth & Power**
to the **Creator YAHVAH.**


## ZARATHUSHTRAN AGE is the Second AGE of man

Essenes of Nazarean (on Mount Carmel) lived thousands of years prior to Zarathushtra, who observed and taught their teachings as symbolised by the Essene Tree of Life.

Esoteric meaning of the Tree of Life is revealed in this book.

Essenes taught the first Messiah, who is YESHUA HA Messiah.

It was YESHUA who preached Love, Peace, the well-known Sermon on the Mount & much more

YAHVAH was worshipped during this Age.

Zarathushtra was the Messiah during this Age who also taught and observed Veganism.

## KALI or BLACK or DEMONIC AGE is the current Third AGE

This is the Age when man dresses in uniform.

Suits with 'fanged' shirt collars & strangling ties (cloth around the neck) symbolising butchery to him for non-compliance of Orders by his Commanders.

Man trains his voice so that his words of deceit are cloaked with words of kindness. Man must sound honest to be successful in convincing unsuspecting people to agree to introduction of new, revised surveillance laws or vaccinations, micro-chip implants, body scanners, finger imprints, bio-metrics or other to enslave man.

Most human beings are slaves and know not.
Man knows not himself.
Man knows not his purpose of Life
Man mimics another,
Dresses like another,
Talks like another,
Eats like another,
Wears cosmetics like another,
Now with social media man follows another
Man is unable to think for himself, Man is totally lost
Man has no individuality
He even speaks words or facial expressions what he sees on TV
Man pretends to believe in some faith or a custom
Because society expects him to observe a religion or tradition
He does not have courage to say tradition has no meaning

Man does not know his original self
Every mannerism is copied of another
He shaves his hair 'short back and sides'- why?

Man is totally blind
Man lives to satisfy the desires of his flesh
Man has no self-control nor any will power
Man has been wrongly taught that he will get crippled with age
Man pays no attention to his Spirit
Man knows not that his Spirit does not die

Man thinks his external appearance is of sole importance
Man thinks he must work 9 to 5
Man wastes his entire Life worshipping worthless money
Money the invisible shackles enslaves humanity

ALL THIS WILL CHANGE
There will be nothing to buy

**This Third Age of DARKNESS is so called, because the Name of ALMIGHTY CREATOR which is ALL POWERFUL:**

**Has been meticulously REMOVED and replaced with the word 'god\*' & the word 'father'**

**The Sanskrit word 'JATAH' from the Vedas which means 'ALMIGHTY CREATOR' is placed in opposition with the Latin word 'patir' 'pater'**

**'ALMIGHTY CREATOR'**

**has now been wrongly changed to:**

**'Father of mankind'**

**instead of**

**'CREATOR of MANKIND'**

16

## Some call their Priests Father!

According to internet search engine 'Wikipedia' the word "Pater is a title given to the father deity i.e. Dis Pater a Roman Celtic god of the underworld...'

## The Vedas describe YAHVAH as

## 'HE who gives breath'

**Western scholars including Max Muller** translates this as:

*'He who sacrificed himself'*

*Instead of*

## 'HE who gives breath'

*None had sacrificed himself. Western Scholars and Jesuits spread wrong teachings since 1893*

**Demonic, Draculian, Satanic Worship to Lucifer accepts Human & Animal Blood Sacrifice**

**Even today some Western Charities still teach slaughter of innocent animals to those unsuspecting in Countries which do not slaughter innocent creatures**

**Cruelty to Human and/or Animal sacrifice must be condemned**

**YAHVAH never accepts blood offering of any kind, be it animal or Human.**

**The English Alphabet 'J' was introduced in 1893.**

**Therefore, for the first time in 1893 the name 'Jesu' was introduced by Western Scholars & 'Jesuits'.**

**The name 'Jesu' represents 'Jesu-its' was formulated by the 'Jesuits'.**

*Reference source of the above for Max Muller & Western Scholars: 'Terminology of the Vedas and European Scholars' by Pandit Guru Datta Vidyarthi, M.A. Professor, Physical Sciences, Government College, Lahore as published in 1893*

There are two forces which surround us - Good & Evil.
The latter opposes the **Natural Law** of YAHVAH.
It is clear that **YAHVAH & HIS DIVINE BEINGS** are strongly opposed by those who have removed **HIS SACRED NAME.**

Through such false teachings the entire world population has lost their Spirituality.

The sole purpose of false teachings is to oppose Morals, Ethics & all that is good, pure, spiritual in accordance with the Natural Law.

The world is controlled by Evil ones. Every conceivable teaching taught to mankind is a deliberate falsehood in order to prevent Human Beings from obtaining Eternal Salvation.

The Sole Purpose of this Channelled Book is to convey Truth to those ready to receive it. It will be only Seekers who will obtain this book which contains both theory as well as practical methods how to accept the Invitation which is the Key to Heaven.

**It can only be Evil Ones who have deliberately blinded global populations, removed & changed the name of the Almighty Creator from:**

## YAHVAH   to   Yahweh

YAH-VAH    to    Yah-**WE**-h

English dictionaries DO NOT have the SACRED, DIVINE name
YAHVAH
English Language changed    `VA´    to    `we´
The alphabet    "V"    came first.
The    "W"    came into existence later.
When  `W´  was introduced,  J,  U  and  W  were not used by the
Romans.
They developed "**J**" from the letter "**I**" as in "ISIS" less than 150
years ago.

**During the current Kali or Demonic Age, Demonic Powers
refer to `YAHVAH´ as a god and not the CREATOR.**

The word 'Create' means to make something out of nothing.
English dictionaries have inaccurate meaning of the word CREATOR.

The word 'CREATOR' has been wrongly replaced by the word 'god'
which is a title similar to Mrs. Mr. Lord etc. as mentioned in the
previous Lesson.

The Almighty Creator is no longer worshipped by major religions.
Places of worship never use the word 'Creator' but only 'god'.

Some religions teach that instead of calling on the Holy name
**YAHVAH** they have concocted names which they say symbolises **HIS**
personality, because their ancestors observed this falsehood,
everyone observes blindly. Others have replaced the all Sacred Name
**YAHVAH** with false names beginning with an English Alphabet which
came into existence in 1893.

Others have deliberately removed the name of the **Almighty
Creator** under the pretext that the name was too holy to utter
replacing it with the word `god'.

**YAHVAH is referred to wrongly as a `god' of the Hebrews**

# NOT the CREATOR of ALL

**During the 3<sup>rd</sup> Age Western scholars insisted in translating Sacred Sanskrit Vedic texts into English. Alongside they introduced the one world religion globally along with education centres, international media etc.**

**Prior to the 18th century there were no religions.**

However, today, centuries later, the source of deliberate false interpretations & teachings are now uncovered.

Misleading teachings have been accepted by millions and are still accepted by millions, who are at the brink of loosing Eternal Salvation and will have to continue further cycles of Reincarnation.

An example, populations use the word 'god' and think they are praying to the one they have in their heart. Another word is 'meat' which originally meant the fleshy part of fruit. The original word 'Milk' too refers to the white juice from plants, herbs, nuts not animal.

Human beings need to understand that it is a Life Style of sincerity to all, love & truth which is required not a religion.

You are responsible for your own Spirit. Your Body is your Temple or your Church. If you have to go to a building to pray, then the one you pray too must be very small to fit into a building.

No priest or man made technology can save you. You alone must work towards saving your spirit. All the guidance you require is in this book.

Prior to the 18th century, Man was Free. He travelled across continents without passports. He did not require money. Entire Nature resources were free, plentiful & pure.

# LESSON 3

## INTRODUCTION TO THE ONE NATURAL LAW

### ONE LAW of YAHVAH is in all life

The   ONE LAW   is in the entire Kingdom of the Almighty CREATOR

It is our inherent natural instinct to desire happiness and love.

We desire to be happy and content irrespective of financial circumstances and worldly possessions.

A baby goes to sleep with contentment, when caressed, fed and loved.

We chase that which we consider will bring us happiness. We do not stop to consider how long the potential happiness will last.

Man made products can provide us with temporary excitement and joy.

One may desire a certain game or clothing, some equipment or holiday or even a specific friend and feel confident this will bring lasting happiness till the game becomes old fashioned or breaks; clothing becomes faded or you have outgrown its size, the holiday has ended or after spending much time with another, one has eventually got bored, the novelty has worn off.

All things man made are temporary. Therefore temporary possessions can only provide temporary enjoyment.

Should you say, ah, yes, but if I could buy a most expensive car or house, or win the lottery then I will be independent and have permanent happiness. Money can never purchase happiness.

Sooner or later your car and house will loose its charm and you will want something else to replace it. All which brings temporary happiness must give us pain.

Billionaires commit suicide or drug addicts because they are bored and unhappy. Happiness is from within.

We recognise that which we know.
When we do not know, we cannot recognise and hence ignore.
You see your friend in the street, you acknowledge him.
You pass by several others in the street and ignore them.
Everyone else is a stranger, who you have no interest in because you are too busy even though you walk down the street, your eyes are blind, your mind is unconscious or your mind is with your technology.

This book will help you to be alert, aware, conscious at all times so that you not only enjoy every moment including passing strangers but most importantly control your internal self through awareness.

So where does happiness come from?

True, happiness comes from within.
Happiness is Peace,
Peace is from within.
Peace liberates you.
Peace gives you Freedom from the invisible chains that have tied you into its invisible web of iron.

Man must awaken, to learn how to break free. This book will set you free with Truth.

Understand that human beings are Spirit beings,
Clothed in Flesh and Blood,
Acting our part, or playing a game.
The play or the game will soon be over.
Will you be the Winner or the Looser?

Below is a simple, basic exercise to assist you to understand yourself from within.

It is best to write down your first thoughts as you do this exercise to help you understand your inner self.

## EXERCISE

Make time to get to know yourself from within.
The best way to get to know yourself is to be silent.
Remove all distractions including your phone and television.
Close your eyes. This will help concentrate by what you see or hear.
Then relax and sit comfortably.

This is called REFLECTING or CONCENTRATING or FOCUSSING by others MEDITATING. It is the Action which matters not the Word.

Many are petrified of the word Meditate.
Meditating is likened to seeing the dirt so that you can gradually commence cleansing.

The best way to describe Self Reflection is similar to writing a letter or replying to an email or some document.

You need to:
Focus,
Let your thoughts flow to you;
Write as the mind flows and your heart connects
Whatever you write will be your words based on your thoughts and/or experience and/or memories.

You might decide to prepare a Draft which is simply having gone through the first process and ashamed with oneself, you have a deep desire to Reform.
This is also beneficial.

During deeper Meditation/Reflection whatever you see is your own self, your own energy or your own spirit.

You will only see that of which you are capable of handling.
Should the thought scare you that is a sign you need to remove all
negativity and balance your thoughts so that positive thoughts are
more prominent than negative ones.

Back to the Exercise.

Your Mind will start to talk to you.
Your Mind is always accurate.
Your Mind will always say the Truth.
Ensure your interpretation is accurate.
Your Mind could tell you about the wrongs you have done to others or
perhaps your Mind will remind you of the wrongs others have done to
you or remind you of some regret or a sad event, it might remind you
of action you need to take.

Your Mind is like a close friend who is constantly concerned about
your welfare and will only tell you the truth.

As soon as your Mind brings a thought to you with negative emotion,
hear it, accept it, release it.

Do not ponder on it.
Should you need to take action either remember the thought or write
down or record a word to help you remember.

Accept the "Headline"
Do not open and read the full thought, you already know the detail,
which brings you much sadness.

Accept the "Headline" that you did wrong.
Send your thought to the person(s) and ask forgiveness.
This is possible only once you accept that you have wronged
someone, and now you are sorry.
Now you have love.

Observe the results.

Next time when you focus, this thought will not come back. Should you meet this person, you will find they will be friendly towards you.

Continue till all your thoughts are removed.

Continue to clear your mind till eventually after removing layer by layer, your mind will have no more negative/baggage
Now you can make progress.

Conversely, you may be the victim of injustice.
Irrespective of whatever the situation might be, you need to forgive.
Only when you forgive then you too can be forgiven.
When we hold grudge, regret, bereavement, grief, sorrow, anger, jealousy, stress, anxiety, hatred, fear, greed etc. these are all negative emotions which are parasites to ones energy, making one lethargic, causing pain, ageing, sickness, disease eventually death.

Positive Thoughts and positive Feelings, Emotions such as love, joy, compassion, forgiveness, release, contentment, acceptance feeds, nourishes your entire body.

As you sit relaxed, in a comfortable position in silence, when your thoughts of the wrongs which others have done to you, come to your mind, send your thoughts to them and say:

"This is the past,
It is irrelevant to me now,
I forgive,
I release,
I do not want to even think about this any longer."

Any thoughts about a sad event, a loss of some kind, send your thoughts and say:
"I thank you for my experience
 This is the past
 I release
 I move on to strengthen my Spirit".

Now move on to the second stage.
Send your thoughts to the Almighty Creator
who is of Purity, Love, Peace and Harmony much more than we can
describe or know.
Tell HIM that you did not know His Law,
that you believed your religious leaders for instance taught and
preached truth.

Have they preached:
1  Keep Holy the Sabbath which commences from Friday Sunset to
Saturday Sunset ?
2 Are you aware that eating Flesh and Blood of innocent creatures is
against the Natural Law?
3 Are you aware trading on Sabbath is against the Law?

Buying & selling is never done on Sabbath by Children of Light, by the
Brotherhood who are also referred to as the appointed ones
messengers or Yesrael which modern English Scholars have translated
as Israel the Country Israel which became a Country in the 1940's.

*Days have been changed by the Beast. The Beast and his numerous*
*Demons preach falsehoods.*
*These Demons or the Beast who is the Head, has introduced*
*opposition Law for Humanity who obeys without questioning.*
*The Natural Law has been changed by the Beast.*
*Names have been changed by the Beast.*
*Teachings have been changed by the Beast.*
*The mark of the Beast is Demonic Worship*
*Demonic worship is only possible to those in Darkness*
*those who have no time for their Inner Self or Spirituality.*

Ask the Almighty Creator for guidance, ask any question regarding
your spirituality, you will mysteriously receive the answer(s).
It is recommended to write your questions so that you can tick them
off when you receive the reply as well as thank the Sole Creator,
YAHVAH.

# LESSON 4

The One NATURAL LAW
The Never Changing Law
The Never Updating Law
The One Law for All Life

It appears that during this technological age
Man lives an unnatural life
Man is unaware of the One Natural Law

You are Spirit Beings
You are Actors
You are NOT living in Reality
(though you think you are)

Life is like a Game
Observe the Rules & you win
Or else
You start the Game all over again
Do you really want to be reincarnated?
Do you wish to have Eternal Happiness on another Planet?

Question     What is Reality?
Answer       Reality is all which is Permanent
             That which is Permanent never Changes
             That which is Permanent never Ends
             That which is Permanent is of Truth
             That which is Permanent never requires Updating

Question     What Proof is there that I am Spirit dressed in Flesh &
             Blood & Muscles & Skeleton etc.?
Answer       Spirit feeds Spirit
             Your Breath is Spirit.
             Without Breath you become Spirit.
             Food from Plants feeds your Flesh & Blood.

| Question | What is Spirit which feeds my Spirit? |
| --- | --- |
| Answer | You are alive because of the Air you BREATHE |
| | Stop BREATHING |
| | & You are transformed. |

Your Spirit will leave your Flesh & Blood
Your Spirit never dies
Your Spirit lives forever

All life has Spirit
All life Breathes
Because you are Spirit

| Question | Where will I go when I leave my flesh & blood? |
| --- | --- |
| Answer | This depends on your life style. |
| | You will receive your rightful justice. |

Question    For how long will I be on a Planet?
Answer       Put it this way, all those who commenced deceiving the
world, your ancestors in the 18th Century, with false Religious, false
Teachings, removing the name of the Almighty Creator
from Scriptures & Places of Worship,
have only recently received their rightful justice.

It is approximately 25,000 years depending on several scenarios.

| Question | Scientists say, there is no life on the Planets. |
| --- | --- |
| | Is this True? |
| Answer | Planets too give off radiation which effects all life. |
| | Only that which is of life can emit radiation. |

Human Beings have no understanding of Planets & the Divine
Archetypes responsible for the operation of Planets. Neither do they
understand the very planet they live on.

These Archetypes are Created by YAHVAH
These Archetypes worship YAHVAH
Everyone must worship YAHVAH

We give reverence to the Archetypes

Question    I do not want to go to the Planets.
            I want Eternal Life.
Answer      Then observe the Natural Law –
            Accept the Teachings
            Cleanse your River of Life
            Accept the Invitation with the Keys!

Question    I have eaten Flesh and Blood all my life, so have
            my ancestors. What proof is there that it is harmful to
            my Body?

Answer      You will observe that every individual who
            celebrates cruelty, who supports slaughter of
            innocent creatures:

MUST be sick or diseased
MUST have weak sight, defective hearing
MUST have High Blood Pressure, suffer from the heart, have blood
disorders, lack vitality, have premature aging, arthritis, gout,
Alzheimer's to name a few.

It is impossible for them to have Perfect Health & Peace.
It is impossible for them to have Spirituality.

Question    Where is the Natural Law?
Answer      It is everywhere. All that is both Visible as well as
            Invisible.
            The Natural Law is in all Life.

Question    What is the One Law?
Answer      It is the Greatest Power from ONE Source,
             the SOLE CREATOR.

Question    Where can the One Law be seen?
Answer      YAHVAH commanded the Sea to remain within its
Boundaries

29

YAHVAH commanded the Sun to follow its path.
To Rise & Set according to Seasons

YAHVAH commanded the Moon follow its path to Wax and Wane effecting ALL LIFE

YAHVAH commanded your Heart to be the pumping station of your Body.

YAHVAH commanded your Breath to maintain regular preset temperature of your body.

Every minute Cell has LIFE has YAHVAH'S INTELLIGENCE.
These are only a few examples which no man can change.
These are only a few examples which no man can dispute.

Question    Is the Law ever updated?
Answer      The One Law is of TRUTH.
            TRUTH never requires updating.

Question    Is the One Law of Life?
Answer      The One Law applies to ALL LIFE.
            That which applies to ALL LIFE,
            That which Feeds ALL Life Must be of Life.

Question    How can we learn about the One Law?
Answer      The same way you ask me the Question, in like
manner ask the Cosmos by sending your thoughts.

Question    I have asked the Cosmos but I get no reply.
Answer      Ensure that you tune into the correct frequency, the
correct wave length/Wave band.

Question    How do I tune into the correct Wave Band?
Answer      By creating High Vibrations.

The Cosmos is unreachable by/with Human Technology. Hence, only Highest Vibration can reach there.

| Question | How do I start? |
|---|---|
| Answer | Commence with self purification. |

| Question | What is self purification? |
|---|---|
| Answer | Elimination/removal of every negative THOUGHT, |
| | Never a single Un-truth, |
| | Perform Actions which are Sincere. |

Do to everyone
Do to those who are in need
As you would like to be done to you
If you were in their place.

Sincerity in Thought, Word and every Action
Forgiveness to everyone
Irrelevant of whatever the circumstances might be

Then you will increase your Vibrations

| Question | Will I easily know when I have achieved this level? |
|---|---|
| Answer | There is no doubt that you will. |
| | The One Law speaks to everyone |
| | Obedience to the One Law |
| | Showers one with Peace |
| | Peace to ones Mind. |

| Question | What is the benefit of Peace to ones Mind? |
|---|---|
| Answer | Only at this point one Creates Superior Vibrations |
| | Several other benefits include |
| | Perfect Health, |
| | Intuitive Power |

| Question | How can I achieve Highest Cosmic Consciousness? |
|---|---|
| Answer | It depends on your level of desire |

Cosmic Consciousness is in the Cosmos

Worldly, Earthly Vibrations are at Terrestrial Level on Mother Earth.

Question    Can I help another achieve Cosmic Consciousness?
Answer    Each individual is responsible for his own Spiritual attainment which is achieved though ones own effort.

Question    How can I have perfect thoughts which I find difficult to control?
Answer    Look at everything
Look at all life
Look at every Human Being
Look at every Animal etc
With Love
With Compassion
Do not support slaughter to animals
Do not be envious, jealous or say lies
Be kind to all Life
LOVE is the answer
If you LOVE
You will automatically be TRUTHFUL
You will automatically be Protective
You will automatically not support Slaughter
You will automatically not support War
You will automatically not support Harm in any Form
Observing a day for remembering War
Is supporting War
Is supporting bloodshed
This will therefore attract bloodshed/death to your loved ones. If those in War had limbs amputated, this too will happen to you or your loved ones.

Love is of the Highest Vibration
Love is not Sexual
Love is not Lust nor Lustful Desires
Which Consume your Energies &

Reduce your Vibrations
Unless your sexual activity is for genuine desire for Procreation.

| | |
|---|---|
| Question | What happens if I have sex and use a contraceptive? |
| Answer | With each ejaculation |

Life if Ejected
Depriving Life to Live Sperm is
Depriving Live Sperm of the Right to Live
In other words, one has committed Murder
Taking pills and tablets to prevent contraception too causes disease
These are Spiritual Crimes as well as harmful to your body.

Contraceptives are not safe, they are permeable. Many who use Contraceptives have contracted diseases such as HIV/AIDS which is on the increase

| | |
|---|---|
| Question | Will I be Punished in my next Life for having sex for Pleasure? |
| Answer | One is punished also in this Life for Sexual Pleasure/Gratification. |

Prolonged, discarding of Sperm leads to a Feeble, Weak, Lethargic, Diseased Physical Body.

Besides, there is a set quota of Healthy Sperm to produce children. Once this Healthy Quota is consumed, though one might be able to reproduce, children are likely to be sickly, diseased, lack of intelligence or with weak immune systems.

Such is the Natural Law.

| | |
|---|---|
| Question | Am I supposed to live with my husband/wife and not have sex if I do not want any children? |

Answer          Every Action has a purpose.

                Our pro-creative organs are there for generating Life.
                One can have sex, though without an ejaculation or
                else
                You loose your higher vibrations
                You loose your energy/vitality.    Ended 1:20 pm

LESSON 5

## INTRODUCTION TO YOUR BODIES

## YOUR BODIES

Human Beings are aware of their Physical body.
Most Human Beings are unaware of their Spirit.
Having formed in ones mind an image which is thought of as beauty,
a shape, features, colour or size etc
Thinking it is important to camouflage ones face with cosmetics
or dye one hair,
Not realising all things unnatural harm the body

It makes no difference to anyone other than oneself
Whether one is grey or green or purple haired
Unnatural 'blood' red lipstick indicating the signs of times

Cosmetics, lipsticks, hair dyes are absorbed by the skin and enter the
blood stream.
Labelling on some Cosmetics state or will state that they are not
tested on animals. The European Cosmetics Nuclear Disposal project
funded by the EU launched globally grants permission for nuclear
waste to be incorporated in Cosmetics & Toiletries.

Women think it is necessary to unnaturally push ones breasts up
with wired or bone underwear.

Is it any wonder why breast cancer is on the increase?
All things unnatural eventually cause disease.

If ones breasts were to stand up, like ones nose it would have bone.
Yet society does not think. All follow, all copy blindly. All feel pressure
to conform.
Be yourself.
Only those of intelligence can be themselves.
Be different in compliance to the Natural Law.
If you lack self confidence then only you feel the need to conform.

The unnatural design of High heels results in unnatural pressure on
your internal organs causing disease, feet deformity etc

Focus not on external features
That which alters with age & time
But rather on your beauty from within

Purify your THOUGHTS - ACTIONS - EMOTIONS
Then you will reap the reward of being balanced and in line!!

Cosmic Cosmetics you will receive
Preventing aging, regenerating your Body
With a glowing skin
Certainly not artificially with technology

It is impossible for Man made technology
To assist in ones Spiritual Well Being

Unless you purify your Bodies
You will have every reason to Fear

Man made technology can make you ascend
Into the Black Holes above you will go
Packed with Evil ones by the galore
Waiting for their companions
Into emptiness and darkness
There you will remain
For a few centuries and in great pain
Then you suffer and regret

Here is an analogy of the above.
A child is given hormones, as is the case, in the flesh, blood and dairy
produce which enables cattle to grow unnaturally bigger in order to
produce more flesh & blood and milk.

These hormones enter the blood stream of consumers resulting in
taller individuals. Though taller than their peers, they might be able to

bluff their age, as they will also mature quicker. However, their mind set can only be according to their actual chronological age.

The same is with Ascension.

Unless ones 'Bodies' are purified and in alignment,
One cannot enter the Spiritual Cosmos,
Man cannot bluff his Spirituality

Though through man made technology
One might be able to ascend
You will enter the Black holes
Where you will be tormented by evil ones
From where there is no return.

LESSON 6

## Importance of your Bodies

### YOUR THINKING –
### YOUR ACTING –
### YOUR FEELING BODIES
### YOUR AURA &
### DISEASE

## YOUR THINKING BODY

Be KIND to receive KINDNESS

Be compassionate to others
So that you too will attract compassion unto yourself

Try to understand you Inner Self
Instead of trying to understand Others

You are responsible for your own Thinking Body
Think Thoughts of Sincerity Always
Thereby, all will also be Sincere with You

Think Thoughts of Deceit
That is what you will attract from others

LOVE all so that you may also attract & receive Love

Spread your Peace from within you

Greet everyone with Peace
Without touching another
Then you too will receive Peace

We attract to ourselves

38

That which we are from Within

Love is the chariot
Driven by Harmony
Love removes all discord
Increasing your Vibration
With your every Higher Thought

Your Mind forms Thoughts
Thoughts are a superior force
Your Thoughts grant you permission
Allowing you to say and do
That of which you Think

Thoughts are superior than your Actions
Thoughts are superior than your Feelings

Thoughts form your Energy body around your Physical body
which is called a Force or Aura which can also be seen by the trained
naked eye.

Higher Thoughts or superior thoughts form lighter Vibrations
rise above the terrestrial plane.

Utmost highest Spiritual thoughts are the lightest
They float into the Cosmos
This is how we receive Spiritual Thoughts
It is said that all thoughts have been thought of before

Every contributor of Thought
Has the Name of the contributor

If you steal anything,
Including Teachings/Knowledge from another
And claim it as your own
If you sell this Knowledge
& promote it as your own
You do to yourself utmost damage

Whereby double-fold the amount of money you make
Will be taken away from you
Because you have stolen
Besides you will also observe that others will steal from you

Hence Credit must be given to the Initiator of Teachings
This is Truth
This is also not having a false ego
This is Sincerity

Thoughts direct ones Feelings
Thoughts direct ones Actions
Thoughts help us Justify our Feelings and Actions
Though not always accurate

When ones Thoughts are of Superior Vibration
And your Body is totally Balanced
You will be able to see the Great, Pure Archetypes
All Created by YAHVAH, the Sole Creator

As a Spiritual Human Being
You will be able to see the Archetypes not only through ones third
eye, which is Located between the two eyebrows, referred to as the
physic eye but also through your Naked Eyes!!!

What is Invisible to some is not really Invisible but rather Reality!!!
This equally applies to Thoughts.

Perfect your Thoughts
To bring your physical body to balance

Remove every negative Thought
Remove every negative Emotion
Remove every negative Feeling
Remove every negative Action/Deed/Word
Remove ones big Ego
Remove all worldly Attachments

It is also wrong to consider ones-self superior due to Spiritual achievement for example.

Never look upon anyone as inferior should they be unable to grasp Spirituality. Just consider them embryos or babies who will one day grow up and become conscious. This might take several lifetimes. Hence, each one of us must focus on our own individual Spirituality.

Nurture others. Never force any beliefs or Life Style upon anyone. You will never be successful.

Depending on ones evolution one either accepts or rejects.
This is not a problem.

This book too is simply to 'Sow' the seed in those who are ready.
If one is ready, one will accept

Alternatively, one will be unable to even read these pages nor accept these words. This is fine. We all evolve as Human Beings at different rates. That is all.

Obstacles will come and remain.

You will accept only when you are ready

I reiterate, one cannot force anyone to change their Life Style

These words are all about a Life Style. A Life Style whereby some in Ancient Days were prosecuted, because the Life Style is about Love to All, Peace within & Justice which stems from the Natural Law, compiled and Created by the Sole Almighty Creator,
YAHVAH.

YAHVAH reigns For Ever!!!

## OUTSIDE INFLUENCE

### How to judge if the influence from another is good or evil?

A simple method is to think
Will the influence
Result in something good which will enhance my Spirituality or
Result in that, which, I will be pleased to disclose to the world
Or will the result of the influence make me feel ashamed
that I will hide and not disclose to anyone

Always judge the result of the influence
By the Result of the Action
Anything which you wish to hide
Anything which is evil
You need to have the courage and will power to reject.

Now since your intent for purification has commenced
You will initially receive tremendous temptation. Be aware!

## YOUR ACTING BODY

Develop your Will through your Mind controlling your Words and Actions

Try fasting or try to skip a meal or simply do not have that cup of Coffee.

We evolve, always, only as Human Beings
From lower to higher consciousness
Human Beings were never Monkeys or other animals
If that were the case then the species would be extinct with the evolvement of Human Beings

As we evolve, we first become considerate to others. The next stage is we become conscious and develop ethical and moral standards.

We loose our selfish ways becoming aware of our Spiritual energies which effect our Physical body mechanism.

We are all currently evolving - the momentum is speeding. Whatever anyone does effects another either directly or indirectly. If someone is angry or in pain, their negative vibes are around the lower spheres absorbed by the unsuspecting negative THINKER!!!

We must all examine our own conscience, and rectify ourselves. After all, we can only change our selves, we cannot change anyone else, neither can we ever change Government & Scientists which are here to enslave Mankind. They too are enslaved.

The good ones, awaken and soon resign since the Human Race is always exploited by each other, economically, oppressed by him politically, suppressed by military force. This will never change as long as there is Government.

Once the Human Race awakens and realises that he, himself, is attracting oppression onto himself through his own inharmonious Thinking, Emotions and Actions, then, and only then will there be Peace & Prosperity.

Harmony is Solely though compliance to the Natural Law. Disharmony to the Natural Law results in Disasters, not sent by the Almighty Creator, No, definitely not, but Solely deliberately Man Made. Disasters, including Earthquakes can all be predicted.

We are responsible for our own actions.

Constant awareness of ones Actions
Constant awareness of the Results of ones Actions
Will soon make one immediately aware of that
Which one should NOT continue thereby reform our Actions.

Genuine Actions of kindness and love to all life brings about Peace and Harmony from within, to the performer.

Peace and Harmony cannot be purchased it can only be gained.
It can only be earned.
Peace and Harmony are gifts
Create high Vibrations resulting in healing, which will cure your body.

Thereby, every disease can be prevented, including the false diagnoses of cancer & deliberate man made pandemics. The word cancer means, 'we do not understand the disease'.

Sadly, the majority do not know that every disease can be cured through Cosmic Healing which is Free.

This is why there is the educational system with diverse professions to enslave mankind.

## FEELING BODY

Create a Will power by abstaining from that which bothers you
That which leads you to temptation
With determination you will succeed
Then temptation will desert you
Temptation will go where it knows it will be successful

Temptation is anything which will result in blocking your purification

Emotions are extremely powerful
Negative Emotions cause people to lie
To Blackmail another is a serious spiritual offence.
Only when one is controlled by Evil Thoughts
Resulting in Evil Emotions
These Evil Emotions will give rise to Evil Words
Emotions cause one to decide when and what to eat for instance

An example of The PROCESS

Your every Thought is first Justified though your Mind
Only once your Thought has been Justified
For instance your Thought has allowed you to feel hungry
(not solely by your body clock)
Your Thought may also Justify a specific taste of food or a drink
which only lasts a few seconds on the tongue yet man is a slave to
taste.

This Justification is sent to your Emotional body
Your Emotional Body coordinates with your Acting Body
Now your Acting Body performs the Action

The purpose of this channelled script is to create awareness or
Spiritual consciousness within yourself, so that you take control of
your EVERY Thought, Word and Action and realise that they are ALL
born within you forming a habit.

The habit could also be the type of taste, the type of sensation on
your tongue by eating flesh & blood, the emotional state by drinking
alcohol. Numerous examples can be given.

Therefore you have to control your Bodies
Through your Will, though your determined Thought

Only you are responsible and only you can control your Thoughts
(though there is Mind Manipulation technology which manipulates the
weak minded person to become a terrorist for example. They perform
the Action which is out of their character. They might not even know
that they have performed the killing. This is what happens with Mind
Manipulation which is on the increase. Hence, you must protect your
precious Mind. You are your Mind.

Negative actions need to be removed
Since every negative Action
Produces negative Vibrations
Every negative Vibration will eventually lead to Disease

Whatever you Do in life
Whatever you Say in life
Whatever you Think in life
Be it good or wrong is all recorded
In your unique book of life - your Aura!!!
It is this which you cleanse when you Meditate

Thoughts, Words and Actions, all effect your vibration

Body liquid is a result of ones Emotions.
Emotions either form Energetic Energies resulting in Positive Emotions
Alternatively lethargic Energies based on negative Emotions.

Though your Aura is invisible to some, your Aura can also be seen by
the naked eye of the Spiritual person.

Similarly, though you may think your Thoughts are secret only known
to yourself, that is absolutely wrong. Your Thoughts are heard by the
Spiritual person even across continents there are no barriers.

LESSON 7

## A Healthy Body is a Healthy Spirit

## How to protect your internal body functions

It is vital to protect your internal body functions to assist you achieve Cosmic Consciousness.

## BODY TEMPERATURE

Your healthy body will regulate a steady heat of 98.4 degrees Fahrenheit

Increased temperature when having a fever results in the alchemical process.
They change the toxins by burning the virus, bacteria thereby cleansing your blood.

When we consume whether by eating or drinking anything which is hotter or colder than ones body temperature, it causes an imbalance within the internal organs.
This is unnatural.
This imbalance causes cells to die rapidly with replacement not being possible, should consumption of such foods be regular.
This cannot be replaced artificially but solely manufactured within ones guts.
Artificial replacement results in disease.

## BODY CELLS

Every single cell within your body is created for a specific purpose, to perform perfectly by transmitting signals throughout the entire body, including internal organs and nerve transmitters.

Consumption of solids and/or liquids either colder or hotter than ones body temperature kills the natural bacteria in your body.

Over time this excessive heat destroys the nerve transmitters thereby causing numbness, pain, malfunctioning of an organ, loosening of the gums resulting in ones teeth to fall out, bloating or swelling of ones stomach, leading to eventual death of an organ, limb or other.

It is vital to feed every cell to obtain its specific food though plant life.

## BODY FUNCTIONING

Every tiny part of the body has a purpose and function including important ear lobes, the navel and the tongue which sadly man pierces causing irreparable damage to specific internal body organs which will not be covered here. Perhaps later, in a medical book should that be the inspiration.

Whatever you put into your mouth including tooth paste is absorbed into the blood stream, hence the importance of reading the ingredients.

It is equally important to understand your skin, which is the largest organ of your body. Whatever you put on your hands for example, immediately enters your blood stream.

## FALSE CLEANLINESS

It is of concern to observe the increased popularity of liquid disinfectants used for the hands.

Sadly, water and ordinary soap is no longer recommended nor used.

Carry disposable gloves, which you can reuse instead of that which will enter your blood stream.

Disinfectants are labelled as hazardous chemical. However, disinfectants are also used in liquid soap which when on the palms of your hands and rubbed are immediately absorbed into your blood stream entering every organ in your body. Your palms also represents every organ and sense in your body.

## FOOD TEMPERATURE

Anything hotter than the temperature under your tongue will damage the internal organs in your body.

Have you ever seen a bird with a bloated stomach or pecking at hot food. Birds, creatures of the wild have a Natural Instinct and automatically observe the Natural Law.

They never seek cooked food nor hot food when it is Winter, even during coldest winter. Yet man has 'ice cream' in Summer not realising the damage to ones teeth, gums, throat and all the organs in the body.

Ice Cream is popular because of its publicity and tradition without any Thought. Ice Cream cannot cool the body though a cold shower can.

## MANS UNCONSCIOUSNESS

Birds never allow their feathers to be cut.
Their feathers trap warm air, help them regulate body heat during all seasons as well as their balance etc.

The natural shape and form of the eyebrows too have a specific purpose.

Hair on the head improves body strength, regulates the temperature on the head also protects the head and brain.

Proper care for ones body is by not overeating.
Always leave space in your tummy so that you can have at least another apple for instance.
Overeating destroys VAYU/Air within the stomach, causing digestive AGNI/Fire to be extinguished resulting in indigestion and formation of carbonic acid gas which poisons the body.

## IMPORTANCE OF LIVE FOOD

Hot food is heated food, is cooked food, is mainly dead food without nutrition.
Your body cells are alive.
Live body cells are fed with, are nourished with live cells from fruit, which grows on plants/trees and ripened in the sun.

Human cells comprise of various minerals including copper, iron, potassium, magnesium, vitamins, calcium, iodine which are all found in the juice i.e. the cells of fruit if they are non- genetically modified, non-genomic, non- transgenic.

Sadly UK Scientists & Universities, in collaboration with Pharmaceutical Organisations, NHS partners all receive funding from Collaborative partnership globally through the EU to remove heirloom i.e. perfect Nutritious Fruit, Vegetables, Herbs through Genetic, Transgenic or Genomic Engineering.

This is how the Economy is strengthened. This is the greatest Crime against not just Humanity but all Life. Birds too who eat of this fruit drop dead.

This is why the Foods Standards Agency, who is also involved in the above label the above produce with 5 a day warning. Unless Human Beings become more active and involved in these Consultations, you will be diseased and so will your children who are now having their four limbs amputated as infants.

The Natural Law made our body out of the same substances of nature. Our body cells are nourished by Plant Life because our body cells are made and nourished by Mother Earth despite what New discoveries scientists might proclaim.

Ever wondered who is responsible for Mental, Diseased Individuals and adult nappy wearing nation. It is my intent to reverse this downward spiral.

Vital nutritional minerals are found deep within PRITHI/Soil which is absorbed by the roots of plants and transported to the blossom, the fruit for man to enjoy.

## HAZARDOUS CHEMICAL FOOD

Scientists & the food industry sadly have modified fruit and vegetable plants reducing and in many cases removing their vital nutrition resulting in the weakening of your immune as well as nervous and circulatory body functioning,

When your immune system is weak, this will show on the weakest part of your body first.

Scientists and all those in the Food Sector have deliberately inserted viruses and bacterium, into plant DNA in the name of Sustainability to kill pests. When pests eat the produce they die.

What therefore then happens to Human Beings who eat the produce?

It does not end here, they have also inserted foreign/alien DNA such as reptilian, mammalian, avian, insects, scorpion, slugs serum etc etc to name a few. This is why Strawberries, Tomatoes, Blueberries, Cherries, Plums, Bananas etc do not rot.

They simply become hard like brick if you leave them outside the fridge for over 6 weeks.

Papayas, Mangoes, Avocadoes etc have been reversed engineered so that the outside remains hard and firm, enticing you to purchase the produce whilst the inside is rotten.

The above equally applies to a wide variety of products sold in your Super Market.

In reality there is no more Plant species. Hence soon Plants will not grow. For this reason, seedless fruit is being sold.

Now there are Printers which print layers of chemical flavours to taste and look like appetising fruit. This is sold as read to eat, pealed, sliced packaged fruit. It has never been grown.

This results in unknown diagnosable diseases to Human Beings whilst also destroying PRITHVI/Soil rendering Mother Earth barren.

Should you observe the instructions in this book, such unforgivable offences to Humanity and all life will not harm you.

Man can only get what he deserves.

It takes approximately 6 months to see improvement in your body, once you turn Vegan.

# LESSON 8

## Your AURA

Your Thoughts, Words and Actions form your Body Vibrations.
Your Body Vibrations form your Aura.
Your Aura surrounds your Body and can be seen by the trained naked eye.

Whatever you think is never forgotten. It is embedded around your body forming what is called your Aura. This equally applies to whatever you say and whatever you do.

It is therefore vital to think good thoughts, kind, compassionate thoughts, not thoughts of anger, revenge, jealousy, hatred, regret, sadness or any other negative thought.

Never try to scheme deceit.
It will only come back with vengeance to the schemer.

Never Lie.
Always uphold Truth irrelevant of the consequences.

A single lie wipes out ones integrity.
Integrity is of greatest value.
It can never be purchased.
Once lost is lost forever.
Such is reputation.

Involvement with sexual passion movies including pornography burns the nucleus of your body cells, forming sexual lust desires forming indelible images on the brain which are difficult to erase.

Read the previous Lesson on your Bodies - THINKING - ACTING - FEELING and release such thoughts.
Create your Will Power.

Imagine how embarrassed you will be once others become aware of your addiction.

Train your Will to shun that which no longer serves you.
Once awakened you automatically walk away from your past.

Depraved Emotions forms sickening Aura around your Body which eventually leads to sickness

Once you release such desire you will immediately feel uplifted.
Your entire nervous system if diseased, will start to function properly thereby leading to a healthy body.

You are responsible for your own thoughts.

Maintain refined thoughts so that you attract refinement.

There are two opposing forces evil, black, demonic powers and good, pure spiritual powers. Both compete for your EVERY thought, word and action.

Evil rules the world
Wickedness controls the world.
Man is chained with invisible shackles and knows not.
Man has been taught that he is only a Physical body & he believes all his channels of education.

Man is unaware that unless he makes connection to his Divine Self within he will be punished.

Man will loose the game and will have to start all over again i.e. be reincarnated.

One can only make connection with ones Divine Self through Purity.
Therefore Purity is rewarded.

Man will only get what he deserves.
Such is the Natural Law.

In one word, the easiest way to achieve purity is to be conscious of Love for ALL LIFE.

Treat everyone, as you would like to be treated if you were in their place.

There is no greater Emotion than Love.

Where there is light, darkness disappears
Light is Power
Darkness is deceit
Darkness fears Light
Darkness tries to instil fear.
It is only by forming fear within Society and Communities darkness can introduce greater control.

Ones Thoughts, Words & Deeds produce Vibrations
They all have density.
The denser your Thoughts
The lower they descend
Dense Thoughts are around your Physical Body
They seep into your nervous system causing pain, sickness, disease.
Light as well as dense Thoughts, enter your Aura which surrounds your Physical Body.

Your Emotions too have density
Dense Emotions descend and surround your body penetrating your nervous systems causing pain, sickness, disease. Both Light and dense Emotions too enter your Aura.

Since Thoughts give rise to Actions.
Actions are automatically recorded in your Aura.
Negative actions too surround your body penetrating the liquid within your body, affecting the cells within your Body.

Hence the importance of uplifting ones Thoughts, Actions and speaking words of truth, love and kindness. Try not to have any expectations of another. Try not to judge another. Observe maintain your distance if necessary.

## TERRESTRIAL LEVEL

Now you understand that nothing which you Think, do or say is forgotten but rather is around you as well as visible!

The Almighty Creator is truly so intelligent having also created such a mysterious Human Body which is greater than the greatest computer.

The camera was manufactured after scientists found out the working of the eye. Pneumatic equipment was developed once scientists found out the operating of the human body and much more.

Besides surrounding you, your thoughts form clusters at Terrestrial Level.

Have you observed how when you smile, another will immediately return your smile. A smile is light weight a Thought of cheerful disposition which floated and attracted that which is similar.

## COSMIC LEVEL

Everything moves,
Everything is alive,
Everything rises
Depending on its weight

Higher Thoughts which are superior Thoughts or Vibrations rise to the Cosmic Level.

When you think Spiritual Thoughts, asking for Spiritual clarification, the reply is sent either directly to you, or through a Messenger or book or other which you will be directed to.

The Cosmos always responds. Hence it is vital to write down your questions, so that when you receive the answer, you thank the Cosmos and also monitor your spiritual progress.

It is also important to understand that whatever you view on TV has an effect on your Thoughts, Emotions and Actions. TV screens emit negative electrons into your dwelling absorbed by your body. Modern flat TV screens have built in surveillance to record and transmitted externally. The same applies to the Modern cars.

Repetition of anything results in one accepting and considering it natural though once it was considered uncouth and rejected.

Now you accept that which you once rejected as low, evil or of darkness.

All which is man made is promoted through false claims. For this reason, the marketing of a product which is sold as a cure today, will be banned tomorrow.

This definitely applies to blood thinners prescribed to millions which renders blood in the body useless. Blood thinners also destroy the organs in the body.

Man made pandemics including Cancer can also be reversed through 'YAHVAH Curing' which is Cosmic Curing.

Cancer literally means we cannot identify the disease. It is then registered to your Ancestry history linking you with Cancer. Henceforth, you, your children, your grandchildren will all be told they have Cancer. This is wrong because it is false.

However, this is what Society accepts.

In the 1960's when tight jeans were introduced and promoted in movies, etc. our parents, grandparents where outraged, labelling jeans as vulgar. This is because our parents wore modest pleated trousers, never showing the shape of their bottoms. Now, everyone wears figure hugging jeans, not giving it a second thought. In fact, I suppose you too, who read these words might be shocked, thinking there is nothing wrong with jeans.

The point that is made here is how through media, as well as constant repetition, things unacceptable are now taken as norm.

This is how society looses consciousness of ones moral and ethical values. Society does not know the word modesty.

Vibrations are energies which surround our Physical Body.
Good pure thoughts create high Vibrations.
Negative, unkind, deceitful, evil thoughts form low Vibrations.

Vibrations are also referred to as body Chemistry which can be experience in a crowded room, or walking down the street, you might glance at a stranger and find them attractive. It has no connection with external beauty but rather the Vibrations which found similarities. It is the body magnetisms which are compatible.

They form an Aura, the Energy Body around your Physical Body. They duplicate your Physical Body which can be seen by the trained naked eye as well as photographic Kirlian technology, which I believe is incorporated in surveillance cameras as well as body scanners at airports etc.

Human Beings have equal potential to achieve whichever level of spirituality they desire depending on ones dedication.

No matter what your Spirituality might be today should you have deep desire with sincere regret of past wrongs you can climb great heights depending on your commitment.

This being the age of awakening, which commenced on the 21st December 2012, there is an increased number of individuals who are searching for Spiritual Truth.

There is a time for everything.
The time to release this edition is now.
It will be available only to those who are ready to evolve to the next level.

It is impossible for this book to be read by any one who is a non-seeker of higher Spirituality.

As you can agree, this book is basically about your Body as you have never known it.

It is non religious neither can it be termed as paganism.
Religions are man made not just to control you but sadly to steal your Eternal Salvation.

You are divine spirit beings having a terrestrial experience.

The Cells in your Body can vibrate to the highest level to reach the Cosmos. However, this must be achieved through Spirituality not through man made technology or else you will ascend into the evil, alien Black Holes. For this purpose Scientists have developed this technology. You have been warned.

We are all here for a specific purpose. You will soon find the specific purpose for your life on earth.

Complete your purpose of your life on earth, to receive high vibrations for Eternal Life.

Cosmic forces radiate around us and remain dormant within us.

All religions accept death i.e. departing of spirit from body as normal. This is wrong.

Spiritual masters and great yogis in the past ascended as human beings, as Ascended Masters and Messiah's into the Heavens. They never died i.e. they were NOT transformed from flesh and blood into Spirit.

In accordance with the Natural Law, the never changing, the never updating Law, everyone who dies i.e. is transformed into Spirit is automatically taken to the Planet to which they are compatible. It is impossible for anyone to return to earth in their current form definitely not in 3 days. It is against the Natural Law. None can ever return back to Mother Earth in their same form.

When ones spirit leaves ones body, in human terms 'death', this is confirmation that one has not achieved ones highest Spirituality.

Presumably, you have heard of Ascended Masters including Yeshua Ha Messiah who ascended. The sermon on the Mount and many of the great teachings were by Yeshua Ha Messiah who was taught by the Essenes of Nazarean on Mount Carmel who were a Spiritual Sect in full compliance to the Sacred Law of YAHVAH, the sole Almighty Creator. This Spiritual Sect were persecuted by the Romans & forced to hide underground for centuries.
They have now re-surfaced to spread Truth to the World proving that YAHVAH reigns for forever.

These Channelled words of Truth are for man to understand true purpose of his Human Life on Mother Earth.

It should be normal to perfect your physical and Spiritual bodies to attain the level of Spirituality which you so desire.

Peace to your mind for reading so far.
Peace to your Body for your Desire to increase your Spirituality.

# LESSON 9

## Divine Terrestrial & Cosmic Archetypes

YAHVAH, the sole Creator, created ALL Life including Terrestrial as well as Cosmic Spirits.

By invoking Spirits of the physical or visible realms of the Earthly Mother in the Morning, we receive vitality, strength as well as ability to regenerate and heal/cure our Bodies.

In the evening we invoke the Divine Cosmic Spirits who through constant weekly repetition we achieve Cosmic Consciousness.

There are 7 Terrestrial Archetypes who are invoked on each day of the week in the morning and 7 Divine Cosmic Archetypes for each day of the week in the evening.

Each Spirit is invoked by concentrating or meditating upon the specific Spirit whilst contemplating their purpose in your life.

These teachings were practised since ancient times and are of highest truth as you will soon experience.

We are all aware that we are surrounded by Air.
The name of the Spirit responsible for Air is VAYU.
We are all also aware that if we do not breathe, when someone takes their last breath, they in human terms 'die' though that is really not the case, they are only transformed back into spirit.

You never die.
Spirit never dies.
You are Spirit because it is spirit which maintains you and keeps you alive.

Without Spirit you are transformed back to Spirit.

Spirits are also referred to as energies or elements or forces
Depending on ones level of Spirituality one either feels energy, or
witnesses the Archetypes.

Spirits prefer to be called by their actual original name which is a
name in Sanskrit. They do not like to be called by translations such as
Air for instance instead of VAYU.

The Almighty Creator formulated the language Sanskrit, which is
mentioned in the previous pages. Sanskrit is compatible with the
organs of speech. Sanskrit is the Natural Language.

I have tried to mention, where possible, their actual Sanskrit name of
the Archetype alongside the English meaning, so that you can invoke
them using their actual name.

Now since you are aware of the above, as well as the effect your
Thoughts, Emotions and Actions have on your Bodies, it is these
Terrestrial Spirits who when invoked in the morning who will
strengthen the cells within your physical body, thereby cleansing the
water within your Body, gradually curing and healing you - totally
FREE!

Thereafter, you are NOT ONLY cured but also protected!

It is vital to get your Bodies in alignment as well as to maintain this.

Proof that they are of highest truth is that with time, dedication and
commitment you will find you are completely cured and/or of vitality.

Should you wear spectacles, you will not require them.

Mans purpose on earth is to reach Cosmic Consciousness. Man must
understand the Power and Purpose of these great Divine Spirits who

sustain us. We must also constantly work in harmony with them. Only then ones life can prosper. These are vital words to remember at all times.

The Evening invocations are to the Heavenly Cosmic Spirits contemplating their power, force and use in your life.

Below is a list of the Terrestrial as well as Cosmic Spirits.

Both the Terrestrial as well as the Cosmic Spirits correspond with each other as shown on the following pages.

Day starts at Astronomical Dawn.
Day ends at Sunset.
Between Sunset and Dawn is Night.
Night is for Sleeping.

| Morning Terrestrial Divine Spirits | | Evening Cosmic Divine Spirits |
|---|---|---|
| VAYU/Air | Friday | Almighty Creator YAHVAH |
| Earthly Mother | Saturday | Eternal Life |
| PRITRI/Earth | Sunday | Creative Work |
| ATMAN/Life | Monday | SHANTI/Peace |
| Harmony | Tuesday | Power |
| RAVI/Sun | Wednesday | Love |
| JULLUM/Water | Thursday | GNANI/Wisdom |

Our every thought, emotion and action requires energy.

Our bodies require six spirits in the morning and six in the evening to be physically healthy, as well as to attain Cosmic Consciousness.

63

Here are the Corresponding Divine Spirits

| Almighty Creator YAHVAH | Earthly Mother |
|---|---|
| Spirit of Eternal Life | Spirit of Earth |
| Spirit of Creative Work | Spirit of Life |
| Spirit of Peace | Spirit of Joy |
| Spirit of Power | Spirit of the Sun/Light |
| Spirit of Love | Spirit of Water |
| Spirit of Wisdom | Spirit of Air |

Your Human Organs in the Centre of your Body receives the Energy from these Divine Spirits & Archetypes through invocation.

Once you experience the benefit it is recommended you spread the word to as many Human Beings as possible.

The Object is to raise Global Vibration with Harmony, Peace & Love so that we can remove Darkness, remove turmoil and stop disasters.

There will be no place for Darkness to hide. Darkness is automatically converted to Light.

You are Cosmic Beings, created from the ingredients of Mother Earth, & kept alive, maintained through the Great Universal Being, the Great Universal Spirit who can take any Form or any Shape. HE will come down to Mother Earth in Human Form.

It is HE who gives you the Spirit of Life, your Breath.

It is HE who has given every human the Key to Ascend into Heaven. The Key is in the invitation given to man by the Archetypes. They all give you the same message.

Then take the Key and place it in the Lock.

# LESSON 10

## Introduction to Your Terrestrial River of Life
## INVITATION which are the Keys

The main stream of your Terrestrial River of Life flows through the centre of your body near your Spinal Column distributing vital Life Energy to every cell in your body.

The Spirits from Mother Earth are eager to help heal you, cure you. They can only assist you when you obey the Natural Law.

They invite you to receive perfect health conditional you comply to the Natural Law.

All Pure terrestrial as well as cosmic Divine Spirit are created by YAHVAH. They all worship YAHVAH.

YAHVAH is the Sole CREATOR of Love & Purity which is difficult for humans to comprehend.
Without HIM there is nothing.

Without HIM you cannot exist
Without HIM you will not receive your Breath of Life through VAYU/Air.

YAHVAH makes it possible for the sky, the planets, Mother Earth and the entire Universe to proceed with absolute regularity daily.
Without YAHVAH there is no Life, no Intelligence in Life then all crumbles. All requires Breath to Live.

We take Breath for granted never grateful.
Learn how to be grateful to the sole Almighty Creator.

YAHVAH created Powerful Perfect Divine Spirits & Archetypes.

They certainly do not have wings. Neither do they have feathers.
Perhaps the evil ones have wings and feathers, this I do not know.

Divine Spirits have low density
Hence do not require wings

All Divine Spirits have great warmth
They are always willing to help
And are patient and understanding
They have their own departments
Yet they all speak with one voice which you will understand when you
read the following pages.

Develop high Vibrations in order to achieve Highest Spirituality.
High Vibrations will make your physical body become lighter than
Vayu/Air enabling one to float like Spirits, to perform distant healing
and much more, which some refer to as miraculous.

There is no such word as a miracle. Everything is possible through
Cosmic Spirituality. It is this Truth which has been deliberately hidden
from entire Humanity.

Some religions have Saints. This is because the religious leaders,
Popes, Bishops, Priests do not understand Spirituality. They do not
have perfect health.

It is through the power of Purity ones every wish becomes reality.
This is possible because your wish goes to the highest realms
To those who have total control
Enabling the impossible to be possible

Such is the Power which makes RAVI/Sun to give life & light to all
living creatures and plants,
Such is the Power which facilitates CHANDRA/Moon to Wax
Such is the Power PRITHI/Earth to bring forth plants from the Soil.

Spirits are everywhere

Spirits are all around you – which type do you attract?
Spirit is within you
It is Spirit which sustains you
Yet Human Beings ignore their Spirit and only look after false
appearances.

Spirits have various forms
There is a Divine Spirit of Life - which is within and around you
There is a Divine Spirit of Power - which is around you
There is a Divine Spirit of Air - which is within and around you
There is a Divine Spirit of Water - which is within and around you.

Divine Spirit of Water is also the
Divine Spirit of Air in another form

Divine Spirit of Air gives you Life
Therefore the Divine Spirit of Air
Is the Divine Spirit of Life
Is the Divine Spirit of Water
Which is the Divine Spirit of Power

They all speak with one voice
Air is Life is Water is Power
They are all fluid
They all contribute to the flow
They all assist your River of Life or Tree of Life
They are all individually extremely powerful
They all send the same message

Are you beginning to see the Picture?

You are not your appearance.
You are basically 'C E L L S' with a nucleus
Therefore, you are mainly Water!!!
Your skin is the bag which holds it together
Preventing leakage of 'cells'

The next pages begins the words of your Invitation of the Key to Heaven which is the Key for Eternal Life. This means that you do not die. You do not leave your physical body on earth. Instead you ascend into Heaven above like the Ascended Masters.

In order to Ascend you must be light.
You become light through controlling and perfecting your every Thought, your every Word & your every Action.

Nothing which you ever say, do, or think is lost.
Everything is recorded.

The great recorder is your very own Mystical Astral Body.
Everything is recorded around your Physical Body.
This is called your Aura or Shield of protection.

Human Beings are superbly designed and created.
Human Beings are connected to the all.
Human Beings effect and affect all.

Human Beings are unable to enjoy the Free World we live in.

Enjoyment is only for a fortnight during ones Vocation or Holiday.
Sadly, this is what man has imposed upon himself.
We have been 'Born Free' to roam, travel both mentally through Spirituality as well as Physically.

Human Beings can only blame themselves.
Slavery is self-imposed.

Free thyself to fly into the Cosmos.
You do not require aircraft.
Let your Spirit show you.
This is possible when you spend more time developing your Spirit through Invocations. Accept the Key.

LESSON 11

## 7 Terrestrial River of Life INVITATIONS or KEYS

Only through Perfect Health you can attain Spirituality.
Irrelevant of your current Health, observe the Natural Law
& Invocations to be cured.

Step No. 1 You must first attain Perfect Health
Step No. 2 Only then you can attain Cosmic Consciousness

### PEACE WITH THE KINGDOM OF THE EARTHLY MOTHER

### Key from Earthly Mother

### Saturday Morning Sabbath invocation

### Divine Spirit of MOTHER EARTH speaks to man:

"I send all my Divine Spirits to grant you energy and health.
I come to you and give life for your whole body.
Your body comprises the elements from the Spirit of Earth,
Absorbed by roots of trees and plants
It is these elements which nourish your body through plant life.
Plants cells are alive
They all have a nucleus.

The same is with the cells in your body.
They too have a nucleus.
They are therefore fed by the cells of plant life from fruit.

Eat my fruit
Chew your food well. Mix your food with saliva.
It is then immediately absorbed into your blood
Receive and absorb the energy from fruit received from the Sun.
With live food
You will eat less food.
Live food is raw food when the cells are alive.

The air which you breathe is born in the heights of the Cosmos
Your breathe is my breathe

The hardness of your bones
Is from the minerals and stones
Your bones are my bones

Your flesh is from fruit which turns from green to yellow to red
Your flesh is my flesh

The water in your body is from the juice of fruit
Water falls down from the sky

The Natural Law makes all which is heavier than Air
Fall to the Soil

My shape is like a disk
I am flat on top with raised Mountains and Hills
Below are the valleys
Each valley has an everlasting Spring of Water
For all life
Your water/blood is my water.

Water always flows down
This is the Natural Law
Water never flows up unless heated
Water flows freely, always seeking its own level
Sleeping in the Underground storage reservoirs
Travelling through permeable layers of filtration
In doing so cleanses and removes all dirt
I purify all your water

The Sun has the keys for the gates of the Horizon
Enters the East of your country in the morning
While exiting from the West
Simultaneously enters the East of another country
Then allowing you to have your rest

Constantly moving from East to West
To North to East
In a never ending journey

Your Bodies require pure Air, clean water, fresh fruit,
Earth to grow things
As well as Earth to walk on
The sun to make things grow
And sweeten fruit
You must live in harmony with all life to be healthy.

I rule over your body
I formed your face
None will ever look like you
I always create new faces
That which exists now
Will never return again
That which existed now
Never was before

I maintain you
I preserve you
I embrace you
You cannot part from me
You are in me
I am in you

Maintain your Body according to my Law
Maintain your Spirit according to the Law of the Creator

You & I are one
I give you the food of Life
For your whole body"

# LESSON 12

## PEACE WITH THE KINGDOM OF THE EARTHLY MOTHER

### Key from PRITHVI/Divine Spirit of Earth

### Sunday Morning Invitation & Invocation

### PRITHVI/Divine Spirit of Earth - SPEAKS TO YOU

"I am a messenger from the Earthly Mother
I come to you as life generating force within your body

From tiny seeds grow herbs, giant trees & other plants
As the mountains erode nutritious dust of minerals
Mingle in my Soil
Precious Minerals & stones
All ground up
To strengthen your Bones
Sent to the roots of plants to nourish your body
Within me are all precious metals
Copper, silver, gold for your immune system & vitality
For you to heal your body and remove all pain
Become healthy and strong again

Do not stray from the Natural Law
I uphold mighty Oak trees
Which no man can endure
I nourish their roots
That they live for Centuries
Be like the Trees
Observe the Law to have Eternal Life

I preserve plant roots and protect them during severe winter

Plough the soil and plant all which nourishes your body
Then your land will be blessed.
I give you a good harvest

I make fertile the wombs of females
That there is laughter of children on my land
Sex is for creation
Sex is for regeneration of your body when you do not have any more
children

Sex is not for pleasure
Sex for pleasure DE-GENERATES your body
Resulting in premature aging
Weakening of your entire body
All which gives pleasure must give pain
Should it be against the Natural Law
Obey the Law

Protect your River of Life which flows within your Body
I am your roots
From me rises the energy within your Body
Roots of man which prevent him from rising
Release, let go
Only then you can rise

Nothing man made matters,
Nothing man made is reality
Nothing man made will remain
Everything man made are the invisible shackles

I am more powerful than all creatures on Mother Earth

Negative emotions unless transformed
Are your invisible shackles
Will cause you pain and grief
Preventing your River of Life to flow

Start now. Heed my words

I will re-generate your body and heal you"

# LESSON 13

## PEACE WITH THE KINGDOM OF THE EARTHLY MOTHER

## Key from ATMAN/Divine Spirit of Life

## Monday Morning Invitation & Invocation

## ATMAN/Divine Spirit of Life - SPEAKS TO YOU:

"I am a messenger from the Earthly Mother
I come to you to give strength to your whole body

I am around you,
I am within you,
I am with you,
I give you Life.

Acknowledge me to enhance your Life,
To extend your Life
Respect and Love all Life so that you too may be loved.

If you support war, fight in war, commemorate war
And lives lost due to your support
Your participation in war,
You will attract misery to yourself & your family
Sorrow which you brought upon others
Such too you will receive
Lives of innocent creatures who cannot speak
In Justice, great calamities you will see

First the loss of your loved ones,
Your children
Then calamities will befall thee
Such is the Natural Law.
We attract that of which we are.
Be of Love
Obey the Natural Law of Life

74

I am in your Breath,
In every tiny cell of your Body
I ignite within your Body
That your River of Life is lightened
When you Love all Life
Resulting in a high vibration
I will grant thee Life, Health & Vitality
So that your Spirit will remain with thee
Extending your days on Mother Earth
Only if that is meant to be

Be conscious of me
I am within you
I am around you
I feed every cell in your Body
If not your Life gradually goes

I am the River of Life which flows through mighty trees
Gives food, shelter and protection to all Life

I am the messenger to Man
Be not ungrateful to the sole Almighty Creator
Obey the Natural Law"

# LESSON 14

## PEACE WITH THE KINGDOM OF THE EARTHLY MOTHER

### Key from Divine Spirit of Harmony

### Tuesday Morning Invitation & Invocation

### Divine Spirit of Harmony - SPEAKS TO YOU

"I am a messenger from the Earthly Mother
I come to earth and give Harmony and Joy to all beings
I am in all Creation

I beautify nature
So that you may enjoy
The delicate buds and petals
Of beautiful blossoms and flower
The gorgeous tiny and large birds
Hear the melodies they sing from afar
Feed them and see the joys which they bring

The aromas of heart warming herbs & tall ancient trees
To give you great pleasure
In all that you see

Walk with nature
I give to you freely
That you may have great joy

Absorb these beauties of nature
The Sunrise and Sunset
Rejoice at the first sign of Dawn

Thank the Almighty Creator
For the great and tremendous Land
For the Hills the Mountains and all the Sand

Observe the Natural Law
Maintain Harmony within
In all that you do

Spread Harmony
Then you will attract Harmony

Harmony is fuel for your body cells
Causing them to increase their vibrations
Harmony cleanses your veins
Removes toxins from within
No High Blood Pressure
No Cholesterol disease
Will be within your Body

Eat of the Fruit of the Tree of Life
For Eternal Joy which I bring
Your days of darkness are over
Into the Eternal Sea your travel begins
Through your River of Life
This is the message of Joy which I bring

Harmony must be gained Naturally
Harmony cannot be gained through Technology
Harmony is earned by your attitude
Harmony cannot be given to anyone
Harmony must be attained by yourself

Never sin again
For your River of Life will flow swiftly upstream"

# LESSON 15

## PEACE WITH THE KINGDOM OF THE EARTHLY MOTHER

### Key from RAVI/Divine Spirit of the Sun

### Wednesday Morning Invitation & Invocation

### RAVI/Divine Spirit of Sun - SPEAKS TO YOU

"I am a messenger from the Earthly Mother
My rays give Fire of Life to your whole body
I strengthen your Bones

I never sleep
I am never exhausted
I produce high vibration
My rays enter all crevices
I remove Darkness
I am of Light
Follow my example
Be of Light
Where there is Light
There is no Darkness
Where there is Darkness
There is no Life
I give Life

Flowers turn their heads and follow me

Eat the fruit which I have ripened
They have absorbed my energy
I change the colour of fruit from green to yellow to golden to red
I make them sweet and juicy to nourish and quench your thirst

I send my rays around thee
Equally on all life without any distinction

Look directly at me with your naked eyes
I will cure thine eyes
You will have perfect sight
I will enter your brain cells

And cure you of your illness
Man hides his eyes from me
Nature cannot harm man
Man harms Nature
Nature protects man
Nature is created with love for man

Look at my face
Observe the many colours around me
Observe how they change
This might sound strange
My magnetic rays will cure thee
I will open the flower within you

I will cleanse the contaminated water within your Body

I have the key for the Horizon
I open the Horizon in the morning
I close the Horizon in the evening
Man sees the Horizon
No man can reach the Horizon
No man can ever know the distance of the Horizon

Invoke me that I may enter your Solar Plexus
I will give the Fire of Life to your whole body
To warm the water within your body
That it may rise
Enabling your River of Life to constantly rise"

# LESSON 16

## PEACE WITH THE KINGDOM OF THE EARTHLY MOTHER

## Key from JULLUM/Divine Spirit of Water

## Thursday Morning Invitation & Invocation

## JULLUM/Divine Spirit of Water - SPEAKS TO YOU

"I am a messenger from the Earthly Mother
I come to you and give you the Water of Life for your whole body
I am the Water of Life in Fruit
Eat me
I will nourish thee as I am in thee

I am in the Oceans, Seas & Rivers
I am strong and mighty - See my Waves
Hear me crash along the sea shore
Equal furrows which I make
My water vapour feeds delicate petals

I am the Most Powerful liquid
Bathe in me
I will heal thee
Drink me
I will feed thee
Use me to wash away all dirt
I will cure thee of all ailments

Evil ones run away from me

I spread light
Obey the Natural Law of YAHVAH
That you too can transform from Darkness into Light
I do not go beyond the boundaries of the sea shore
Fire transforms me into Air according to the natural law

Your Fire causes me to rise
Enabling your River of Life to Flow higher
We attract that of which we are.
Be of Love"

All Life has a very high percentage of JULLUM/Water.

It is vital to understand further body functioning of JULLUM/Water for a variety of reasons:

- So that you could apply this to any pain or disease;

- The important message from VAYU/Divine Spirit of Air is understood

- You grasp the functioning of your Terrestrial as well as Cosmic River of Life

We are now entering exciting information.

JULLUM/Water circulates Nutrition from food throughout the Body hence the vital need to consume at least 50% raw live plant food.

Life sustains life.

Chewing food properly in the mouth, mixing it with saliva, enables nutrition to immediately enter your blood stream even before it reaches your stomach.

JULLUM/Water comprises Red & White blood corpuscles or cells as well as albumen, Plasma, a clear liquid which heals/forms a scab on a wound. Blood Thinning pharmaceuticals are harmful for every organ in your body causing them to gradually deteriorate and eventually collapse. First, your wounds will not heal. Blood has to have a specific viscosity to circulate within your Body.

JULLUM/Water circulates throughout every cell in the body. It is JULLUM/Water which enable you to feel sensation.

Where there is no JULLUM/Water as in our nails and hair, there is no feeling.

When a part of the body lacks sensation, this indicates there is a problem with ones circulation.

As a natural process body cells die and are replaced only with correct live nutritious food.
When JULLUM/Water circulates in your body, it enters every cell in the body, which has a central nuclei as well as albumen which is alive and causes it to Vibrate.

Depending on the frequency of the Cells Vibration it can contribute to pain/sickness and disease or excellent health.

Excellent health is a blessing, a gift. If you do not have health, you need to strive to perfect you 'Bodies' as mentioned in the previous lessons. Should you wish I am always there for you.

With excellent health ones River of Life will flow upwards, through your energy centres causing them to rotate forming greater energy within your Body.

The flow needs to be from your Root i.e. Prithvi or Divine Spirit of Earth to the top of your Head.

This is your Terrestrial River of Life because it goes within your Body.

It is called Life because your physical body will be healed, irrespective of any disease including cancer.

Impurities from your body are removed through oxidation hence the clean blood is bright red and flows through the arteries, whereas the contaminated blood is bluish in colour in your veins which transport blood to the heart. This you should clearly see on the back of your hands.

If your veins are flat and not slightly erect at the back of your hands it is a sign that you need to cleanse your Blood.

You do not need to purchase anything. No tonics or medication.

Simply follow these instructions. Ensure you inhale slowly and deeply as long as possible. This way your intake of oxygen into your body through your lungs will be to its full capacity.

When you exhale, i.e. breathe out, do this consciously. Slowly, Exhale. Let it be long and deep raising your diaphragm. Pull your tummy in at the same time to push the toxins which has accumulated at the bottom of your lungs out.

After a few minutes you will not only feel more energetic but also irrelevant of how weak you were feeling or how flat the veins on your hands were you will see a tremendous improvement.

It is AIR or VAYU which sustains you.
Respect VAYU, be conscious each time you inhale and exhale and you will be delighted with the consequences. After all, it is VAYU who sustains you. You will observe how all are interconnected i.e. VAYU/Air, JULLUM/Water, ATAM/Life etc.

Besides, with clean Blood you have a healthy body.
This is why the Evil ones Poison the Food, Air & Water to make you diseased.

Hope you are finding this as exciting as I am in relying the finer working of your body.

# LESSON 17

## PEACE WITH THE KINGDOM OF THE EARTHLY MOTHER

## Key from VAYU/Divine Spirit of AIR

## Friday Morning Invitation & Invocation

## VAYU/Divine Spirit of AIR - SPEAKS TO YOU

"I am a messenger from the Earthly Mother
 I come to you from the Cosmos to give myself to you the Air of   Life
for your whole body

Only that from the Cosmos can sustain you,
Because you are a 'sleeping' Cosmic Being

Awake! Here, take me freely
I am always around you
I am within you
I desire to be in every cell of your Body
To maintain Life in your every cell
Take me

Inhale me - long - slowly & cherish me
No word can you speak whilst you Inhale me
You have to Exhale before you Inhale
This is the Natural Law of YAHVAH
Sound cometh out only whilst you Exhale

Then you are complete
Such is the Natural Law
I am VAYU/Air I give thee Life
I am inside the organs in your body
To assist your Fire of Life to burn with mighty flames
To digest your food

To give you energy to walk and think
To regulate the temperature of your body
To ensure correct circulation of water within your body
To send vital Life energy to every cell in your body
To ensure there is sufficient energy to flush your arteries, veins and capillaries, without which you will have swelling, numbness, loss of feeling eventually disease.

I bring the messenger from AKASHA/Ether to give you Life Energy, To Awaken you

I give you ATMAN/Life
All Life breathes
Where this is VAYU/Air there is Life
VAYU/Air feeds nourishes every cell in your body

As I nourish every cell in your body,
I cure thee
For a Healthy Body breathe slowly and deeply
Take in oxygen, nitrogen
Take in Life Energy which is Spirit.

Shallow breathing does not take in sufficient Life Energy which is Spirit to energise your Central Body mechanism.

It is therefore vital to consciously breathe deeply, in a clean, unpolluted area.

Do this whilst focussing your thoughts on me,
Meditate on me in silence
Let your mind speak to thee.

Such is the Natural Law
Your Body is created to function through me
I am your Terrestrial River of Life"

# PRAISES TO YAHVAH

Almighty Creator YAHVAH
Thou who was never born
Yet Thou art now
Thou who IS
Thou who will always be
Thou who created all Life
Above & Below, In the Cosmos
In the depths of the Oceans & Sea
On Mother Earth
More than we can comprehend
Thou alone art the Rightful Owner
Thou alone art the Rightful Ruler
Thou art the Sole Creator
Thou art the Ruler & Owner of the Entire Universe
Thou alone has Power over mans Spirit
No man has power over Spirit other than Thee
No man can manufacture technology to harm Thee

Thou who created Powerful Archetypes to enable us to
maintain cleanliness
Water to wash away all direct, in any circumstance
Air to remove offensive odour
Sun to clear the Air and Water
Earth to filter the Water

Who else has so much love for Man
Even though Man ignores Thee

Thou created us that we may have Eternal Life with Thee
What greater love can there be?
Thou created us with extreme Love and consideration
Catering to our every need
Allowing us to choose
Either to obey Thy Law or reject Thee
Thou gives us a reward not just of Eternal Life
But also Peace, Prosperity, Harmony

Whilst here on Mother Earth
Yet man in his ignorance
Rejects Thy generous, irreplaceable abundant gifts
Shuns all that of love, peace and harmony
Turns away from Thee
Then wonders why there is misery, destruction & violence
Sickness, disease and chaos
Which he brings to his own body
Not understanding he himself has attracted turmoil
By rejecting Thee
Thou art of Pure Love
Thou hast sent Thy Divine Spirits with Thy Invitation
With the Key to Thine abode

Come to Earth soon, This I pray
Thou art the ONLY JUDGE for the End Day
Thou alone upholds Justice
Thou alone upholds Peace
Thou alone upholds our Freedom
Yet man turns away from Thee

Thy Will be done always
We praise Thy Most Powerful Name YAHVAH
We Worship Thee and Thou Alone
We Teach & Observe Thy Natural Law
Thou art the Sustainer
Thou art the Preserver
Through Thine Divine Spirits
Thou art the Creator of ALL LIFE

None other is worthy of Worship, but Thee

All Honour and Glory be given to Thee
Thou the Universal Creator
Who has had pity on me
I have been wicked in my sinful ways

Not obeying Thy Law during many of my days
Now that I have found Thee
Now that I know
I Worship & Adore Thee Alone
Thou who supports my Freedom
Enslaved I have been all my life
This I now leave behind me
Working towards my New Life

Thou who always was
Thou who will always be
Thou who created all life
By Wisdom of Thee

Thou the Supreme Being
There is none like thee
Thou who Created us for Freedom
Love, Peace and Harmony

We pray that thou will come soon
Whence in the New World there will be
Never ending Love
We will all Worship Thee

No Messiah will come to make judgement
Thou alone are the rightful judge
Thou who supports sincerity
Honesty Truth and Love

Then Truth will be disclosed
To all man, far and wide
We long for the Age of Justice
Only then we will survive

THOU who is never changing
THOU who opposes every EVIL
THOU who transmitted the Divine Law into all Life
THOU whose Divine Law freely gives all Life BREATH

THOU who CREATED SPIRIT in BREATH
THOU who IS the SPIRIT in BREATH
Yet man knows THEE not - to his long term regret

Where there is BREATH there is LIFE
Where there is LIFE there is BREATH
THOU who created all Life by THY Thought
THOU whose Vibration is in the Cosmos
THOU whose Vibration is the Universal Sound of all Creation
All Life can hear THY SUPREME VIBRATORY Sound
THOU who loves all life as THOU loves all THY flawless
Creation
THOU who is all forgiving
THOU who is all JUST
THOU who abhors bloodshed of any sort
Including lust
THOU who invites us all to THY KINGDOM
Conditional that we have Good Pure Thoughts
Conditional that we have sincerity in all our Words & Actions
Never expecting a reward in return for Kindness
This is all which we require
This is the Esoteric Law

SADLY.....    it is THOU who is ALL Pure ,
              It is THOU who is ALL Just,
              It is THOU who CREATED us for FREEDOM

Yet it is THOU the world knows not.

Sadly, it is THOU, human beings ignore

Sadly, it is THOU, human beings wrongly call god

Sadly, it is THY Holy Law man blasphemes

Thereby killing Himself through his ignorance

Spurning the Golden Invitation of Life
To his eventual destruction & death

I pray the world will soon AWAKEN

& Praise & Worship Thou O Great Universal Being
Thou the Great Universal Being
May there be Justice for THEE
THOU deserves much more that we can give

Thou ALONE created us for FREEDOM
Yet Human Beings choose to be enslaved
Yet Human Beings despise & Ignore THEE

Thank you YAHVAH!
Thank you for my Life
Thank you for my Breath
Thank you for my Health
Most of all
Thank you Thy Love
For the Invitation & Key for Eternal Life
There is no other source which can provide
Love greater than Thine

Justice for Thee
I hope I can bring
Mankind to realise
His folly and then we can sing
Praises to YAHVAH
The Almighty Creator
Who soars above All
For this I sincerely pray
It is clear man is awakening
This will happen soon, One day!

# LESSON 18

## History of Sabbath & the Beast

In ancient times, it was common practice to observe Sabbath commencing Friday sunset to Saturday sunset. Sunday was then the first day of the working week.

However, Pope Gregory, representing the VATICAN, introduced the Gregorian calendar, changing the days of the week from Sunday which was the first day of the week, to Sunday being changed to the 7th day of the week.

Pope Gregory then ordered the 7th day observance on Sunday and not Saturday thereby preventing Holy Sabbath observation.

During the 18th century, anyone in the UK found to observe Sabbath from Friday evening worship to the Almighty Creator YAHVAH was taken to Westminster market and burnt at the stakes. The evil ones are petrified of the power of Sabbath.

The Essenes of Nazarene of Mount Carmel in the UK who observed ancient teachings were forced to flee underground. They have now emerged from their hiding places.

It is observed that every conceivable Law of the Almighty Creator which is of Purity, Truth, Love, Peace, Freedom for all life, Justice to all is opposed by the Beast.

Stealthily, through centuries the Beast has altered the days, times, seasons, teachings, the Law etc. with one sole purpose for Humanity to loose their Eternal Life and continue their cycle of reincarnation.

The sole purpose of this channelled book discloses that which Humanity should know. Heed these words of truth for Eternal Life. Nothing else matters. The Beast will soon be dissolved.

## LESSON 19

## ANCIENT COMMANDMENTS TO CHILDREN OF LIGHT

There is only one such Essene in the UK. The Creator gave the Law
for his people which is a covenant for the Children of Light, also called
Yisrael not Israel. (Israel was declared as a country in the 1940's. The
word Yisrael dates back to the first age.)

YAHVAH's Law for the Children of Light states that only the Children
of Light will be able to accept and observe this Esoteric Law which is
the Brotherhood.

Below is Part of the Law for the Children of Light:

"I am the Law, there shall be no other Laws on any land.

I am the invisible Law, without beginning and without end.

Thou shalt not make unto thee false Laws. I am the Law and the
whole Law of all Laws. If thou forsake me, thou shalt be visited by
disaster for generation upon generation.

If thou keepest my commandments, thou shalt enter the Infinite
Garden where stands the Tree of Life (which I refer to as the River of
Life) in the midst of the Eternal Sea.

Honour thy Earthly Mother that they days may be long upon the land
and honour the Creator that Eternal Life will be thine in the Heavens,
for the earth and the heavens are given unto thee by the Law, which
is the Creator.

Thou shalt greet thy Earthly Mother on the Morning of Sabbath

Thou shalt greet the Divine Spirits of Earth, Life, Joy, Sun, Water, Air
on prescribed mornings.

Greet & consecrate thyself to all these Divine Spirits of Earthly Mother, that thou mayest enter the Infinite Garden where stands the Tree of Life.

Thou shalt worship the Creator on the Evening of Sabbath.

Thou shalt commune with the Divine Spirits of Eternal Life, Work, Peace, Power, Love and Wisdom on prescribed evenings.

These are the Divine spirits of the Creator and thou shalt commune with them that thy spirit may bathe in the Fountain of Light and enter the Sea of Eternity.

Keep Holy Sabbath to receive the Light of the Law.
Search the Light, the Kingdom of thy Creator, do not do any work, on Sabbath and all things shall be given unto thee.

Thou shalt not take the life from any living thing.
Life comes only from the Creator. Only HE who giveth Life can taketh Life away.

Thou shalt not debase love.
It is a sacred gift from the Creator.

Thou shalt not trade thy Soul the priceless gift of the Creator for riches of the world. "

# LESSON 20

## INVITATIONS HOLD THE KEY

### 7 Cosmic River of Life INVITATIONS are the Keys for Cosmic Consciousness

### PEACE WITH THE KINGDOM OF THE ALMIGHTY CREATOR

### Friday sunset is the start of Sabbath Celebration

### YAHVAH the Sole ALMIGHTY CREATOR SPEAKS to the Children of Light.

**"Keep Holy Sabbath to receive the Light of the Law.
Search the Light.
The Kingdom of Thy Creator
Do not do any work on Sabbath &
All things will be given unto thee."**

**Observe the Holy Law
To enter the Eternal Sea
Where stands the Tree of Life
Of Eternal Life**

**This is the invisible bridge
Children of Light build & climb
Forming the link
Between Heaven & Mother Earth
When all the Children of Light have awakened
So will the journey begin**

The above emphasises the Esoteric Law which will only be accepted and observed by the Children of Light who have completed their evolution.

The Almighty Creator YAHVAH created mankind because of Love that we may perfect ourselves so that we may join Him and enjoy his mighty creations.

Because HE is of purity, nothing impure can confer with HIM.

We are on Earth as Human Beings alive through HIS Spirit
Yet know HIM not
Yet we acknowledge HIM not
Yet we ignore HIM
HE who gives us LIFE

We are Created to enjoy HIS Creations
To maintain a Spiritual Life of Truth
To maintain a Spiritual Life of Peace
To maintain a Spiritual Life of Love & Harmony
So that we too Ascend into the Heavens
Once purified & perfected

YAHVAH created the entire Universe in 6 days.
On the seventh day, he looked at his creation and liked what he saw. He blessed this day and said as a sign between the Children of Light and those of darkness, only the Children of Light will observe and keep Holy Sabbath, which is the seventh day, in accordance with HIS Law.

All others will continue buying and selling, without any consideration of keeping Sabbath Holy. We may work for six days i.e. Sunday to Friday. On the 7th day which commences at Friday sunset and ends on Saturday sunset, we are to focus on our spirituality.

Disobedience of this Law is the Mark of the Beast.

This Law was maintained for centuries during the Golden Age of prosperity. Man tended to his physical requirements for six days and on the seventh day he rested devoting attention to his spiritual needs.

Worship to the Almighty Creator is the central prayer.
Sabbath is the totality of all the morning as well as evening invocations.

These invocations teach us that we must become 'Cosmic Conscious' - that our River of Life should flow further into the Infinite Sea where dwells the Almighty.

This is our purpose of Life.

Once we are awakened to cosmic consciousness, we realise that without Divine Cosmic Spirits we cannot survive spiritually.

We strive to comply to the Natural Law perfecting our spiritual body so that we can align with Cosmic currents which are within us as well as around us.

It is vital to unite with the Cosmic Spirits thereby attaining Cosmic Consciousness.

This is possible when we observe the Natural Law and teachings from the Terrestrial as well as Cosmic Divine Spirits.

Only then we can say,

"I & the Almighty Creator are One".

During Sabbath one can continue to increase ones Vibrations by elevating the Spiritual Bodies as explained in the previous Lessons resulting in achieving a higher level of Spirituality and thereby become Cosmic Conscious.

During Sabbath you might consider reading those sections in this book which attract you. Pondering on the inner meaning would be useful. Write your questions so that when you receive the answer you not only say thank you but monitor your Spiritual Progress.

# LESSON 21

## THE KINGDOM OF THE ALMIGHTY CREATOR

### Your Cosmic River of Life INVITATION

### Key from the Cosmic Spirit of Eternal Life

### Saturday Evening Invitation & Invocation

### DIVINE SPIRIT of ETERNAL LIFE speaks to man and says:

"I am created by the Almighty Creator
 Here is your Invitation to your Cosmic River of Life
 I am from the Great Kingdom of the Almighty Creator

This is the Key for Eternal Life
Your purpose of Life is to live forever
This you can achieve
As you Balance your 'Bodies'
Increasing your vibrations to the highest degree
Formulate your Thoughts so that you overcome gravity
Your Thoughts must rise above the Planetary

Love is of the highest Thought
Love creates the highest Vibration
Be sincere without deceit
Be forgiving & compassionate
Have no expectation of another
This is the recommended way to set you free

Look within
Only you know yourself
Only you can purify yourself
Though guidance I give to thee
Tomorrow might be too late
The best time is to start right now

Obey the Natural Law
Sincerity in your every Thought
Genuineness with your every Word and Deed
This is my message
So that you cleanse yourself
And remove negativity

Then you overcome gravity
In your Thoughts, Words and Deeds
Superior Thoughts of highest are required
This is an urgency

You can soar above the clouds
Your Cosmic River of Life too must flow
Into the Heavenly Sea
You will begin to see the Light
Of your own Body"

# LESSON 22

## THE KINGDOM OF THE ALMIGHTY CREATOR

### Your Cosmic River of Life INVITATION

### Key from the Cosmic Spirit of CREATIVE WORK

### Sunday Evening Invitation & Invocation

**DIVINE SPIRIT of CREATIVE WORK speaks to man and says:**

"I descend from the Cosmos, the Almighty Created me
I have an Invitation for you
Which will set you free
Upon humanity the message I bring

I give abundance to all men
Who work with honesty
Who work in accordance with the Natural Law

Those who work to spread the Natural Law
These are workers of Harmony
Who struggle sowing Truth
In an alien society

Work done well, which you have enjoyed
Receives blessings of enormity

Work towards spreading Truth
Be of Light - with delight
Seed planted now
Might take a long time to germinate
Such work is done by the 'Children of Light'

Work with Nature
The inexhaustible source of knowledge
From whence you are rewarded
With energy and harmony

Undertake Work with pleasure
As a means of observing the Law of Nature

Your harvest will be rewarded
With tremendous knowledge and vitality

Observe the cycle of plants
How the phases of the moon
Effect all aspects of your life
That is why there are the Planets
For mankind to see the enormity
Of Creative Work which one can do
Only when one can see

Cleansing your River of Life
Removing all debris
Enabling the flow into the Cosmos
This is your reality

Working on specific times and days
On your River of Life
Your work will be successful
To ensure the flow is uphill
Into the Cosmic Infinite Garden of Life"

# LESSON 23

## THE KINGDOM OF THE ALMIGHTY CREATOR

### Your Cosmic River of Life INVITATION

### Key from the Cosmic Spirit of SHANTI/Peace

### Monday Evening Invitation & Invocation

### Shanti/Spirit of Peace speaks to man and says:

"I come to you to give you Peace
Peace to your Body from the Earthly Mother
Peace to your Spirit from the Almighty Creator
That you accept the Invitation from the Cosmos
When you obey the law
Create Peace within your Mind
It will flow to your actions and words

Peace cannot be obtained through man made technology
Man has deceived you & your ancestors
Walk away now
Since you can see

Create Peace within
Only then you will have harmony
Give Peace to all life
In all situations
Then you too will attract Peace

Peace is the Cosmic Tonic for your Bones
Peace strengthens your immune system
Which no man currently seems to know

Partake not of wars
Or wars will come back to thee
As you do unto others
So will also be done unto you and your family

Evaluate yourself
Contribute your best to Humanity

101

By doing so, your Cosmic River of Life
Flows into the Infinite Garden
When you will soon see
The Fruit which you have planted
Will be there for all Eternity

Peace is vital for spirituality
Walk with the Spirits of Earthly Mother
Observe their instructions
This is how to obtain Peace

Greet your brothers by wishing them Peace
Then you too will attract Peace
To your own body
Peace be with thee."

# LESSON 24

## THE KINGDOM OF THE ALMIGHTY CREATOR

### Your Cosmic River of Life INVITATION

### Key from the Cosmic Spirit of POWER

### Tuesday Evening Invitation & Invocation

### DIVINE SPIRIT of POWER speaks to man and says:

"I am the Spirit of Power
With my source from the Almighty Creator
The Power over all Spirit
The Power over all Life
All of Life has Spirit
All which has Spirit has Life
No man can create Life
No man can create Spirit
No man has power to change this
It all comes from the Sole Almighty CREATOR.

I descend upon your Acting Body
I will direct all your acts.

I come to you as Cosmic Power
I give you Life
Uniting you with Life on all planets

I am within you
I am around you
That you may accept the Cosmic River of Life Invitation

The atoms of Power operate within your 'Bodies'
Only with high vibration - from purity
Awaken now to your purpose of life
That for which you are born
So that your River of Life which flows unto thee
Is thoroughly cleansed from debris

Then you will rise
And move from the world cities of death

Uphold the Sacred Natural Law
Embedded upon your conscience
I am here to help you
Invoke me, when you are ready

A River of Holy Power is the Law
Which will flow from the Cosmos to thee
Praise and thank the Almighty CREATOR
The source of all Power
Now and has been since all Eternity

I have Power because of my Purity
I uphold Peace
I uphold Love
I uphold Justice
Be like me
Uphold Truth

I will give you Strength and Vitality
Uphold Love to ALL ATMAN/Life
Cleanse your Thoughts
Cleanse your Mind
Combine your Actions & your Words
Then you too will have the Power to receive Eternal Life

Such is the Natural Law.
We attract that of which we are.
Be of Love"

## LESSON 25

## THE KINGDOM OF THE ALMIGHTY CREATOR

## Your Cosmic River of Life INVITATION

## Key from the Cosmic Spirit of LOVE

## Wednesday Evening Invitation & Invocation

## DIVINE SPIRIT of LOVE speaks to man and says:

"I am the Spirit of Love
I am the highest creative feeling
Join my Cosmic Ocean of Love
Through your River of Life
Love spreads happiness
From within your Heart
To the aura around your Body
Protecting your health and immunity
This is the secret of well being
Taught to humanity
As is our inner feelings towards others
So shall we attract unto ourselves

Be gentle kind and forgiving
Always with sincerity
This is the greatest source of Harmony

Flush your River of Life with Love
No matter what the circumstances might be
For as we do unto others
So shall be done unto thee

These words are of utmost importance
As you can clearly see
They have the greatest impact on ones Cosmic Vibrations
This is the only way

You can set your body free
From worldly shackles
Into the Cosmos you fly with glee
But never through man made technology
Into Black Holes you will be
For several centuries

Great calamity befalls
Men of deceit
Disease and chaos they attract
Into their Physical & Mental Bodies

I descend upon your Emotional Body
To purify your feelings
Love all life not just Human Beings
Love everyone
Forgive everyone
Accept everyone for who they are

Emotions of Love are the highest vibrations
Do not have expectations of anyone
Give freely never expecting repayment or gratitude
Help everyone in need
Then you will have the highest vibrations
Then you will be able to fly (without wings!)

Love is of the Almighty Creator
Who created man with Love
That man too may enjoy the splendour of above
Love the Almighty Creator by obeying HIS Law"

# LESSON 26

## THE KINGDOM OF THE ALMIGHTY CREATOR

## Your Cosmic River of Life INVITATION

## Key from the Cosmic Spirit of WISDOM

## Thursday Evening Invitation & Invocation

## DIVINE SPIRIT of WISDOM - SPEAKS to you

Spirit of Wisdom speaks to man and says:

"I am the Spirit of Wisdom
With my source from the Almighty Creator
I descend upon your Thinking Body
To enlighten all your Thoughts

Man who thinks goods thoughts will be of Wisdom
Wisdom comes from understanding esoteric Cosmic reality
Termed by man as 'mental'
Because man of darkness is unable to see

Purity attracts Wisdom
Wisdom destroys all negativity
Allowing good thoughts to flow
From the Cosmic Ocean of Thought

Treasure Wisdom once attained
Making your River of Life flow
Into the Cosmic Eternal Sea
From where there is Light
Which shines upon thee
As you will clearly see
Reality!

Think genuine, kind, compassionate Thoughts
Never think negatively
Even though it is true that someone for instance is of deceit
You do not have to mix with them

Alternatively plant the seed in their thoughts for them to
reform
Only when they are ready they will accept your words
Your thoughts are around you
Your thoughts form your Aura
Auras are visible to some
Displaying your entire personality

Higher thoughts reach the Cosmos
That is how I send you answers to that which you seek
The best day to seek is Saturday before sunset
Then I am close to Mother Earth
Responding to all those who seek

Wisdom cannot be taught
Wisdom is earned
Wisdom has the highest vibration
Wisdom has only one Source
Solely from the Almighty Creator"

Use your Mind to create your Will
Will develops integrity
Reflect, concentrate, meditate on your days performance
Daily strive to improve yourself
Maintain a daily record of your Spirituality."

# LESSON 27

## Your Terrestrial & Cosmic River of Life

### PEACE WITH THE KINGDOM OF THE ALMIGHTY CREATOR
### PEACE WITH THE KINGDOM OF THE EARTHLY MOTHER

### United Divine Terrestrial & Cosmic Divine Spirits

### Await your Consciousness

### INTRODUCTION

Now since you have accepted the Terrestrial & Cosmic Invitation you have the Key to Ascend to Heaven.

Through Purity you will rise to place the Key into the Lock.

Dedication, determination, perseverance, daily invocations followed by meditation will raise your River of Life, into the Eternal Sea, where stands the Perfect Almighty!

The exciting process has begun for you who have cleansed Your THINKING - FEELING - ACTING BODIES

Now you experience Reality.

Relax, sit comfortably, in silence, light a candle if you wish, close your eyes, look towards your physic eye which is between your eyebrows.

Let your Mind speak to you.
Accept all which it says
Do not ponder on any words
Listen, heed the message and release
Do not get distracted
Do not give excuses
Do not justify

Continue to focus on your physic eye.

Ensure that your breathing is calm and central.

Everyone will have different experiences since all have
varying evolutionary cycles.

## YOUR UNIQUE RIVER OF LIFE - the PROCESS

Life is not stagnant
Your unique River of Life, is of Life - ALIVE
Your River of Life must be kept constantly flowing
Never stagnant
Your unique River of Life flows through your Body

Pictures of saints are shown with a halo around their head
Only when the Sacred Organs in the Head have opened
You too become a Saint, the choice is yours.

Evil ones on Mother Earth are doing everything conceivable
to prevent you from opening your Spiritual Glands which
must be opened through cleansing your Thinking - Acting -
Feeling Bodies
& NEVER though man made technology.

It is the same Evil ones who are manufacturing Technology to
take you into Black Holes, from where there is no Return.
There you will be with Evil ones for centuries for not
complying to the Natural Law.

It is important to remember that food has a direct impact on
your body function.
Details are on the previous Lessons.

**Where there is Light - There is no Darkness**

Enthusiasm speeds progress
On the first few occasions it might be slow,
But certainly well worth the effort
Make time to strengthen your spirituality
This is all which really matters
Consider reducing the hours you spend watching TV
The less you sleep the more active your brain becomes
The more you spend building your spirituality
The quicker you will reach this climax
Meditation, Concentration must be in total silence, with no
interruption
Silence is the Key

Now the next stage is very important
I hope you will now see
Once your Physical Bodies are all perfectly functioning
Your 'Spirit' ascends into the Cosmos
Receiving Blessings from the Almighty

Hence you must increase your Vibrations
Through your Thoughts, only Naturally
Definitely not using man made Technology
Good spiritual thoughts with total glee
Concentrate on your Permanent life ahead
Rather than that which is only Temporary

Release all your attachments
Love all in harmony
Speak no evil of anybody
Accept everyone just as you see
Judge another only if you too wish to be judged

Your unique River of Life
Is your Bodies energies
Flowing into your Vital Organs
Turning the wheels for Electricity
Understand Cosmic Reality
Just as it is meant to be

*Because YOU are SPIRIT*

*That is why*
*That is how*
*You are alive by feeding your Spirit with VAYU/Air*

*AKASHA/Ether is the Cosmic Energy*
*VITAL for your ENTIRE BODY*

*You have Cosmic Energy within your Body which is dormant*
*The same way you have forgotten your past lives*

*Once you RAISE your VIBRATIONS*
*Thereby OPENING your ENERGY CENTRES*
*You will look back on your existing life style with*
*abhor*

Spirit of VAYU/AIR speaks to man and says:

"I am the messenger of ATMAN/Life from AKASHA/Ether
I am supreme Life Force from the Cosmos,
Created by YAHVAH
My other forms are:
ATMAN/Life,
Power,
JULLUM/Water,
VAYU/Air

I rejoice when you recognise my messengers.

They will lead you to the ONE path
The Path which shows you the way
Where the River of Life Vibration flows
Through VAYU/Air
Because of JULLUM/Water

My messengers guide and assist you
Now you have commenced to climb the path
Continue to put your best effort
Into your every Spiritual Body of Thought

This is the highest vibration
Focus on the one spot
Breathe silently and in balance
Automatically turning your next energy centre

Each energy centre has a specific responsibility
All of them to operate with Love
Nourishing your River of Life with Purity
Kindness, compassion and a good Heart

Your Body Energy Centres
Are your meters like computers
Indicating your Inner Bodies
Give up earthly attachments
Anger, hate & jealousy
Revenge & all negativity
These block your Spirituality

The Second is near your abdomen
Sexual organs and desires of lust
Contribute to negativity
Convert them to feelings of love and trust

Solar plexus is the next one
Above the navel,
Below your chest
Create your Will Power
Then all your food you will digest!

The fourth one is your Heart
Love all irrespective of who they are
Or else circulatory problems will appear

The fifth one is your Throat
Always speak Truth, sincerity and love
Use your Power of Speech
Teach yourself first
Before you try to preach!

The sixth one is your third eye
Between your two eye brows
Develop this power of intuition
Or else depression will occur

Create your Spiritual Will
Confusion then will never come near
This is the seventh
The highest part of your Body

This is the first stage
For Man to progress towards Eternal Life
The Cosmos is inexhaustible
Which no technology can access

Then VAYU/Air
Within your River of JEEVAN/ATMAN/LIFE
And higher energy Centres
Within your Bodies,
Require continued increased vibrations
Now this is your Test
You must do your best
To connect the key to the Lock
You are half way there
Perhaps it now comes as a shock!

One more thing you must remember
Should your concentration fail
Then you need to start all over again
From your coccyx
This might cause you disappointment

The River of Life flows within you
& removes debris
Debris causes blockages and disease
The River of Life can only flow
In Silence when you meditate/focus/concentrate
Or else you will not see

Nothing special you need to do
Just sit and watch the scenery
Sometimes your body might quiver
Which means successful removal of some old debris
Should you rock or sway
Do not be disturbed or dismayed

You will soon know when its over
Should I tell you all the detail
You might misinterpret
And then perhaps fail

Only beneficial Radiation comes from the Planets
From the Cosmos lots of Electricity
Mystical light better than UV
Will cure your whole body

Then the River of Life flows Radiant
Directly from above
Upon thee
From the Supreme Universal Creator
He who always was and
He who will always be
He who upholds:
        **PEACE - LOVE - JUSTICE- HARMONY**
            **For Humanity**
Unity comes only through Purity - In your EVERY: THOUGHT-
WORD- DEED
Then you can truly say:
I & the Almighty CREATOR are ONE!

## Conclusion

Complete Ancient channelled Teachings are not available through any other source. Contact me for further Teachings or Initiation either in groups or individual.

Now the Human race will gradually awaken to accept that you are Cosmic Beings with the Invitation and Key to Ascend into Heaven.

This is substantial Proof that YAHVAH REIGNS FOREVER.

Justice will be brought to the sole Almighty Creator YAHVAH
Justice about His Creations of Divine Spirits to help mankind
Justice about His Mysterious Galactic Power
Truth about His Personality of Love & Harmony

Peace to your Mind for reading to the end
Peace to your Body for accepting the words
Peace to your Spirit for your intent to implement these Teachings.

Now as I end these Lessons
Let us all live together in Peace and Harmony
When you meet your fellow brothers
Introduce them to a Life of Reality
Greet them with words of Peace
By greeting them as such
Peace will then be reflected back to you.

Spread the word about this Book
That they too may have access to Truth
Spread this through your Social Media
So that collectively we can light the Skies
Removing all darkness, removing all devastations
Look within, protect your Inner Self and all things will come to you.
Peace & Blessings
Stella Hermoine Howell   Mobile UK : 44 + (0)7831 220631
Stella@ecotrace.co.uk    www.ecotrace.co.uk

Lightning Source UK Ltd.
Milton Keynes UK
UKOW04f2102180118
316403UK00001B/66/P